Building Trust, Making Friends
Four Group Activity Manuals
for High Risk Students

Peter the Puppy Talks About Chemical Dependence in the Family
(Grades K-6)

by

Teresa M. Schmidt and Thelma W. Spencer

JOHNSON INSTITUTE®

Minneapolis

Contents

Acknowledgments — vi
Introduction — 1

Part One: Establishing a Support Group Program for At-Risk Children — 3

Chapter 1: Dynamics of the *Building Trust, Making Friends* Group Model — 4

    Group Format — 5
    Progression of Themes — 8
    Displacement Communication — 10
    Benefits of Use — 11

Chapter 2: Implementing the Group Program — 14

    Gaining Administrative Support — 14
    Staffing and Training — 15
    Developing Referrals — 16
    Screening Candidates — 18
    Acquiring Informed Parental Consent — 19
    Forming and Scheduling the Groups — 20
    Assuring Group Confidentiality — 21
    Self-disclosing by Leaders — 22
    Role Modeling by Leaders — 23
    Following Up Group Participation — 23
    Using the Program in Guidance Counseling — 24
    Using the Program in Family Therapy — 24

Part Two: Group Guide for Peter the Puppy Talks About Chemical Dependence in the Family — 27

Chapter 1: Issues Affecting Children from Chemically Dependent Families — 28

    The Influence of the Chemically Dependent Parent — 28
    Common Perceptions of Children from Chemically Dependent Families — 30
    The Help that Children Need — 30
    The Role of the Group — 31
    Identifying Children from Chemically Dependent Families — 31
    Understanding Children's Developmental Characteristics — 32

Building Trust, Making Friends
Four Group Activity Manuals
for High Risk Students

Peter the Puppy Talks About Chemical Dependence in the Family
(Grades K-6)

Copyright © 1991 by the Johnson Institute. All rights reserved. No part of this book may be reproduced or transmitted in any form or by any means, electronic or mechanical, including photocopying, recording, or by any information storage and retrieval system without express permission in writing from the publisher:

    Johnson Institute
    7205 Ohms Lane
    Minneapolis, MN 55439-2159

Library of Congress Cataloging-in-Publication Data

Schmidt, Teresa M.
    Peter the Puppy talks about chemical dependence in the family (grades K-6) / Teresa M. Schmidt and Thelma W. Spencer.
        p.   cm. — (Building trust, making friends)
    Includes bibliographical references (p. 231).
    ISBN 1-56246-019-6
       1. Drug abuse—Prevention—Study and teaching (Elementary)—United States.
2. Alcoholism—Prevention—Study and teaching (Elementary)—United States. I. Spencer, Thelma W.
II. Series: Schmidt, Teresa M. Building trust, making friends.
HV5808.S36   1991
362.29'071'073—dc20   91-34249
                                                                                                                                         CIP

PRINTED IN THE UNITED STATES OF AMERICA

92 93 94 95 96 / 5 4 3 2 1

Chapter 2: Session Plans 34
    Session 1: Peter Talks About Chemical Dependence 38
    Session 2: Peter Talks More About Chemical Dependence 48
    Session 3: Peter Talks About Chemical Dependence in the Family 60
    Session 4: Peter Meets Mrs. Owl 70
    Session 5: Peter Learns About Feelings 82
    Session 6: Peter Talks About Anger 92
    Session 7: Peter Learns to Manage Anger 104
    Session 8: Peter Learns Other Coping Strategies 118
    Session 9: Peter Learns How to Take Care of Himself 134
    Session 10: Group Presentation—*Optional* 144
    Session 11: Peter Says Goodbye 154

Part Three: Support Materials 165

Group Rules Contract 168

Feeling Wheel 169

Activity Sheets 170

Basic Facts Worksheets 181

Basic Facts Worksheets with Answers Dotted In 191

Basic Facts Posters 201

All the Basic Facts 220

Audience Evaluation Form 221

Group Evaluation Form 222

Group Certificate 223

Group Award Badge 224

Process and Progress Form 225

Progress Notes 226

Self-referral Group Survey Form 228

Parental Consent Letter 229

Screening Interview Outline 230

References and Suggested Readings 231

Resources for Help 233

Acknowledgments

The authors would like to thank Superintendent Donald S. Bruno and the Pupil Services Department of Newport News Public Schools, Newport News, Virginia, for their support and commitment to substance abuse prevention.

We are also grateful for the willingness of the IMPACT Staff of Newport News Public Schools to participate in the original field testing of this material. Additionally, we offer thanks to the many children who participated in that field testing. Their enthusiasm and ideas enriched the materials.

Gratitude is also expressed to the guidance counselors in York County Public Schools, York County, Virginia, whose suggestions, comments, and questions enriched the work.

Finally, we offer thanks to Matthew and Thomas Schmidt and Leigh Spencer for their great patience and faith, and to Matthew and Thomas as well for their consultation and advice.

About the Authors

Teresa M. Schmidt, M.S.W., L.C.S.W., B.C.D., has been a clinical social worker for nearly twenty years. A graduate of the College of William and Mary and the Smith College School for Social Work, she has specialized in the treatment of children and their families since 1983. Bringing her extensive clinical experience in mental health to the Newport News Public Schools in 1987, she worked with Dr. Thelma Spencer to develop and implement in a school setting a prevention/intervention group program for children from chemically dependent families. Ms. Schmidt and Dr. Spencer conduct training workshops for mental health and school professionals on both the state and national levels. Ms. Schmidt, a Board Certified Diplomate in Clinical Social Work, is in private practice at Oyster Point Counseling Center in Newport News, Virginia.

Thelma W. Spencer, Ed.D., C.S.A.C., has been an educator and counselor for nearly twenty years, working with special populations in a variety of settings. She gained clinical experience in substance abuse counseling while earning her doctorate from the College of William and Mary. Dr. Spencer oversees the Substance Abuse Prevention/Intervention Program for Newport News Public Schools. She is on the adjunct faculty of the University of Virginia and is a consultant for the Southeast Regional Center for Drug-Free Schools and the Virginia Department of Education Alcohol and Other Drug Abuse Prevention Project. Dr. Spencer was honored as the 1990 Outstanding Student Assistance Professional by the National Organization of Student Assistance Programs and Professionals.

The *Building Trust, Making Friends* group model was developed by Ms. Schmidt and Dr. Spencer and was field tested in the Newport News Public Schools, Newport News, Virginia. Through a unique, structured format and progression of themes, the model makes use of clinical and educational theory as well as practical experience to provide intervention and prevention services to at-risk children.

Introduction

Children are at risk. Too many of them. Growing up in homes tinged by the sad effects of chemical dependence,[1] parental separation and divorce, and family violence, these children will face many problems. As a teacher, school social worker, psychologist, guidance counselor, Core Team member, or member of a Student Assistance Program (SAP), it is only natural for you to feel concerned for these children. It is only right that you seek new ways to help them.

You have many wishes for these children. You wish that you could walk with them, be a support to them, be a friend to them, help them in their decision making, keep them safe. You wish that everyone would recognize and see them as special, talented, wonder-filled, precious. Thankfully, many people share your concerns and wishes for at-risk children. More than that, like you, many people are working hard to help turn your concern into confidence and make your wishes come true.

With concerns and wishes like yours in mind, *Building Trust, Making Friends* has been developed for at-risk children from chemically dependent families, from separated or divorced families, and from families in which violence is used to express anger. *Building Trust, Making Friends* consists of four group-model programs. Three of the programs are aimed at children in grades K-6; the fourth is for children in grades 6-8. Each program is based on an eleven-session group model that uses both clinical and educational theory to help at-risk children.

At-risk children share similar beliefs and perspectives. In an effort to create order out of the chaos that is too often so common in at-risk families, the children tend to blame

---

[1] The term *chemical dependence*, as used in this manual, refers to any and all dependence on any and all mind-altering substances, in particular, alcohol and other drugs. Major medical, psychiatric, public health, hospital, and psychological associations have pronounced dependence on alcohol—or alcoholism—a *disease*. The American Medical Society on Alcoholism and Other Drug Dependencies (1987) has officially declared that what is true for alcoholism is true for addiction to other drugs. Chemical dependence has certain describable characteristics. Namely, it is a disease that is: (1) compulsive-obsessive; (2) primary; (3) progressive; (4) chronic; (5) fatal; and (6) treatable. The following may be considered a working definition of the disease of chemical dependence: If the use of alcohol and other drugs is interfering with any area of a person's life—whether social (legal, school;/work, family, or friends) or personal (physical, mental, emotional, or spiritual)—and he or she can't stop using without help, then the person is chemically dependent.

themselves for the problem, whether it's chemical dependence, divorce, or violence. Children also tend to believe that they can control, change, or cure the family's problem. The group model corrects these common misconceptions. Children seem better able to understand new information—information that allows them to change their beliefs—when it is presented in small groups.

The group model also helps children learn how to become aware of their feelings, how to express them appropriately, how to grow in self-esteem, and how to acquire the interactive skills and value systems necessary to function as healthy human beings. The group model engages the children in both the cognitive and the affective sides of learning. It gives the children forums where they can discuss problems and receive age-appropriate information about their family's problem. The group model supplies a safe and supportive environment and empowers the children to grow and heal.

Each of the four programs in *Building Trust, Making Friends* features a format, structure, and progression of themes designed to meet the needs of at-risk children:

1. *Peter the Puppy Talks About Chemical Dependence in the Family* meets the needs of children (grades K-6) from chemically dependent families.

2. *Tanya Talks About Chemical Dependence in the Family* is designed for middle school children (grades 6-8) from chemically dependent families.

3. *Thomas Barker Talks About Divorce and Separation* helps children (grades K-6) from divorced, separated, single-parent, or stepfamilies.

4. *Della the Dinosaur Talks About Violence and Anger Management* is helpful both for children (grades K-6) whose families use violence to express anger and for children who themselves exhibit aggressive behavior.

This complete and easy-to-use manual contains all you need to lead a group of at-risk kindergarten through sixth-graders through the program *Peter the Puppy Talks About Chemical Dependence in the Family*.

Part One of this manual contains materials to help you understand the dynamics of the group model, including group format and progression of session themes. It also provides guidelines and materials to help you implement the program in your school or agency.

Part Two contains materials both to help you understand the issues affecting children from chemically dependent families and to help you identify children from chemically dependent families. It also contains the complete group guide for leading a Peter the Puppy Group. The group guide includes the objectives, necessary preparations, background information and guidelines, and detailed step-by-step session plans for each of the eleven sessions.

Part Three contains support materials, a list of references and supplementary readings, and a list of important resources. This section will further help group leaders and other staff make the group process successful and rewarding for everyone involved.

Overall, this manual provides sound, practical, creative, and innovative ways to help children correct their misconceptions, meet their emotional needs, deal effectively with their problems, and grow to live lives that are much less "at risk."

PART ONE

Establishing a Support Group Program for At-Risk Children

Chapter 1: Dynamics of the *Building Trust, Making Friends* Group Model

Perhaps the most effective and practical setting for this group model is in the school. This is the case for a variety of reasons. First, many families undergoing the stress of chemical dependence or violence deny it and don't seek professional help. Second, even families who aren't in denial often lack the ability or means to make use of professional help. Third, many professional helping facilities, such as treatment centers for chemical dependence, aren't equipped to work with children. Fourth, the organizational structure of many professional helping facilities often doesn't allow people who do have the skills and training to deal with children access to them. Better than any other setting, schools are in a position to offer prevention services—like this program—to the large numbers of at-risk children who would otherwise never receive them.

Schools can offer the group model's services as part of a comprehensive prevention program implemented by pupil services personnel, which include clinical and school social workers, school psychologists, guidance counselors, and chemical dependence counselors. Student Assistance Programs (SAPs) and Core Teams will also find the program's group model ideal to use and easy to implement.

Although the school is a valuable setting for this group model, it may be used elsewhere: in chemical dependence treatment centers that provide family services, in mental health centers, in private practices, and in battered women's shelters.

The same group model is used in all four programs of *Building Trust, Making Friends*. It is a dynamic process that helps meet the needs of children from at-risk families by providing structure, consistency, predictability, and fun. It incorporates a structured format that remains the same for all group sessions. The group model also presents a specific and definite progression of themes that fosters nonjudgmental education about the particular issue at hand, corrects misconceptions that children commonly have regarding the issue, and teaches children effective coping strategies that enable them to let go of futile "overresponsibility" and begin to take care of themselves.

All this takes place through the medium of stories told by either a make-believe animal or a fictional human student. The children can easily identify with these "characters" without feeling disloyal to their own families. The group model enables children who come from families in which they're feeling the severe stress of chemical dependence, parental separation and divorce, or violence to recognize that they're not alone, that other children have feelings just like theirs, and that, above all, they can learn to manage their feelings and deal with them in healthy ways.

Group Format

The group model presented in this manual follows a structured format for each group session that is both educationally and clinically sound. The three-part format includes the same components.

1. Beginning the Session
   - Group rules (reviewed each session)
   - Centering exercise
   - Feelings check-in
   - Review of basic facts (beginning with Session 2)

2. Exploring the Story
   - Story (the heart of the session)
   - Group discussion
   - Follow-up activity
   - Worksheet for reinforcing basic facts

3. Wrapping Up
   - Repetition of centering exercise
   - Affirmation
   - Closing activity

Since the format and its components remain virtually constant through all the sessions, these components deserve a closer look.

Group Rules and Rules Contract. Creating an atmosphere in which a group of children (some of whom might not know each other) feel secure and willing to share thoughts and feelings is a major undertaking. Many children will have never participated in a group process before, so they'll be unaccustomed to the expectations and the boundaries of a group.

Group rules ensure that all group members will be treated with the dignity and respect they deserve. Group rules also establish a standard of behavior for group members. They establish the expectation that children can be responsible for their behavior and their participation in the group.

The group leader presents the rules in contract form and asks the children to agree to them by signing their names to the contract. Rules are displayed in the group meeting room. At the beginning of each group session, the leader reviews them, making sure that the children understand them all. The consistency of this practice reminds the children that they're safe in group, that the rules serve to protect them, and that all group members will behave as they've agreed to behave by their signing the contract.

Centering Exercise. This exercise sets the stage for group work in a positive way. The techniques learned in the centering exercise, which include deep breathing and tensing and relaxing muscles, are not limited to group work only. Once mastered, children can use them in "real-life" situations. Repeated toward the end of a group session, the centering exercise not only reinforces learning but also enables the children to calm down—especially if intense feelings arose during the session—and helps them get ready to return to their regular classroom.

Feelings Check-in. During the feelings check-in the children learn to identify, own, and express feelings in appropriate ways. The group leader validates, accepts, and tolerates the children's feelings. For example, responding to a child who says he wants to hit his mother because she yelled at him, the group leader might say, "It sounds like you're feeling very angry. Can you tell us what you're angry about?" After the child responds, the group leader could continue, "Many children feel angry when that happens to them. But it's important to choose a helpful way to express your anger or to use it to work for you. We'll learn more about anger in Sessions 6 and 7." Again, if a child is tearful because a grandparent has died, the group leader can say, "Many children feel sad or lonely when a grandparent dies. They might show their sadness by crying or by drawing a picture or writing a poem. After a while, they don't feel as sad. We'll learn more about feelings in Session 5."

By accepting and validating feelings and by helping the children identify helpful ways to express feelings, the group leader consistently teaches that feelings aren't bad or dangerous, that they can be felt and expressed, and that they will pass. Thus, the feelings check-in functions both as a corrective and a therapeutic experience for the children.

Review of Basic Facts. Beginning with Session 2, the basic facts learned in previous sessions are reviewed for understanding. This regular repetition and clarification is an effective technique to help even very young children learn and use the key concepts presented in the sessions.

Story (Bibliotherapy). Bibliotherapy simply means "healing story." The story or bibliotherapy uses an appealing make-believe animal (for elementary-aged groups) or a fictional student (for middle school groups) to present basic facts about chemical dependence, divorce and separation, sexual abuse, or violence and the effects of these situations on the family. Most of the children will be able to identify easily with the characters without feeling that they're betraying their family. Even tough, streetwise children experience fun, warmth, and affection with the characters.

Discussion. Each session's story is followed by questions the leader may use to initiate group discussion. In the discussion, the children have the chance to process the story, and the group leader has the chance to make sure they understand the concepts and issues presented.

Activity. Using the Activity Sheets provided, the activity reinforces the material presented in the story. In a nonthreatening way, it encourages the children to express their perceptions of their situation, but only to the degree they can and want to share them.

Basic Facts Worksheet. The Basic Facts Worksheet is a verbal, visual, and auditory tool that reinforces the basic facts the story has presented and the children have discussed. The worksheet is a cumulative learning tool, representing and adding to the basic facts each time the group meets. The worksheet also serves to build the children's positive self-esteem. Unlike worksheets the children might receive in a regular class in school (for example, an arithmetic worksheet), these worksheets are "fail-safe," designed to enable the children to get the "right" answer every time.

Affirmation. This gives the children a chance to end the group session on a positive note, even if intense feelings arose during the session. The affirmation reinforces the content presented in the session and helps the children learn to choose a positive attitude.

Closing. The closing exercise helps the group develop a sense of bonding, cohesiveness, acceptance, and sharing. It allows for physical touch in a safe, nonthreatening atmosphere, which may be a new experience for many of the children. The same closing exercise concludes each session.

This structured format encourages the children to participate as fully as possible in the group process. Go-arounds, where everybody has a chance to describe art work, writing, feelings, and so on, are used extensively to make it easy for group members to share in a safe, nonthreatening way. Although the children are never forced to take part and are given the right to "pass," the format allows each group member at least three opportunities per session to speak and other, non-verbal, opportunities to participate as well. The repeated structure of all group sessions provides a sense of predictability and consistency that is often absent in the homes of at-risk children.

Progression of Themes

The essence of the program's group model is the progression of themes. In Sessions 1 and 2, the program presents the children with education and information about the issues of chemical dependence, separation or divorce, or violence. In Session 3, the program describes how the stresses of chemical dependence, separation or divorce, or violence affect children and their families. Session 4 addresses and corrects misconceptions common among such at-risk children. Then, in Sessions 5-7, the program shifts its focus to identifying, validating, and accepting the children's feelings about their situations. Two of these sessions (6 and 7) help children see anger as a positive force. In Sessions 8-11, the program turns to teaching the children coping strategies, showing them how to detach from futile and overwhelming feelings of responsibility and empowering them, in age-appropriate and positive ways, to take care of themselves.

The themes combine to create a program that helps the children become less at risk, while never making them feel that they're being disloyal to their families. In fact, the group leader never asks the children to reveal negative things about their family, nor does the leader ever make negative comments about people who use alcohol or other drugs, who are separated or divorced, or who use violence. The program consistently describes family members' behaviors objectively and nonjudgmentally. At the same time, the program unfailingly identifies and validates the feelings in children—and other family members—that such behaviors elicit.

Each group program follows the same, specific thematic progression:

Sessions 1-2: Presenting basic facts and information about a specific issue (chemical dependence, divorce, violence in the home)

Session 3: Describing and assessing the impact or effects of the specific issue on the family and the child

Session 4: Correcting common misconceptions

Session 5: Dealing with the feelings the children experience

Sessions 6-7: Managing anger

Session 8: Coping strategies

Session 9: Setting personal goals

Session 10: Group Presentation—Optional

Session 11: Developing a support system

In Sessions 1-2, the make-believe animal or the fictional student presents the children with information on a particular issue such as chemical dependence, divorce, or anger. The character also helps the children identify positive ways of feeling better.

In Session 3, the make-believe animal or the fictional student describes his or her own family, the stress or trauma a particular issue has caused in the family, and the ways other family members have behaved in reaction to the stress or trauma.

In Session 4, the make-believe animal or the fictional student and the children meet a helping professional (Mrs. Owl), who helps to correct the misconceptions common in families affected by the particular issue. Together with the make-believe animal or the fictional student, the children discover that although they can't cure the family's problems, they can do some things to help themselves.

Sessions 5-7 focus on feelings and emotions. Session 5 concentrates on helping the children identify, validate, and come to accept and tolerate their feelings. Sessions 6-7 deal with ways to manage anger by helping the children discover how to express anger in personally helpful ways. They learn to see anger as an energy or power that they can use to work for them, and they learn how to express anger in helpful ways so they can let it go.

Session 8 deals with coping strategies and gives specific examples of situations that at-risk families experience. The children learn about age-appropriate ways to be responsible for themselves and, in particular, how to ask for help when they need it. They also learn how to keep themselves safe, how to avoid assuming responsibility for someone else's feelings or behavior, and how to do good things for themselves.

The objective of Session 9 is to help the children learn how to set personal goals. Children identify ways they can take good care of their bodies, minds, feelings, and choices.

Session 10 is an *optional* session that gives the children an opportunity to offer their own presentation of the many facts and skills they have learned and discovered throughout the group process. When children teach someone else the basic facts they have learned, their own learning increases as does their self-esteem. The children's presentation also helps to raise the level of the audience's learning and awareness, and it encourages future referrals. Audiences can range from a single person—a principal or administrator—to a class of students, to an entire grade level. The presentation is very appropriate for prevention purposes. The group members present only facts. They do not reveal anything personal about either themselves or their families.

In Session 11, the children celebrate their learning and growth. They create their own support system, a "yellow pages," that will help them know where to go and to whom to turn for help when they need it in the future.

Displacement Communication

In its progression of themes, the group model uses a therapeutic technique called *displacement communication* (Kalter 1990)[2] to help children deal with family stress, while allowing them to remain loyal to their families. Lacking knowledge and perspective, children are not often verbal or articulate in describing family problems or their reactions to those problems. Even if children possessed such knowledge and perspective, they still might not want to discuss the problems, both in an effort to avoid or deny their own distress and in an effort to preserve their family's good name. Children are often unaware of their specific feelings and are unable to name them. They're also unaware of their internal conflicts, and end up acting them out by fighting, misbehaving, somatizing, overeating, or trying to be perfect.

Recognizing that children don't communicate directly, the group model also uses an indirect method of communicating with them, by means of a "displacement figure"—either a stuffed animal or a fictional teenager—who tells its story in the group sessions.

Displacement communication contains the following six steps:

1. Represent in the displacement figure (toy, doll, fictional child) the behaviors that signify emotional distress (fighting, crying, temper tantrums).
2. Acknowledge how upsetting such behavior is to the displacement figure.
3. Address the displacement figure's underlying conflict or emotional pain.
4. Correct any misperceptions in the displacement.
5. Accept conflicted feelings.
6. Present alternative ways of expressing and coping with conflict.

These steps are incorporated in the group model's sessions.

In the sessions, in a nonjudgmental way, the displacement characters (make-believe animal or fictional student) are educated about a particular issue (chemical dependence, divorce, or family violence). The characters describe their family stress and their behavior and acknowledge how painful that behavior is. Mrs. Owl, the helping professional, identifies the underlying conflict and the emotional pain common to children in the characters' situation. She then corrects their misconceptions and misperceptions by teaching them the three Cs: children don't cause and can't control or change parental chemical dependence or divorce or violence. Mrs. Owl goes on to teach the characters how to identify, accept, and express their feelings in appropriate ways. Finally, she teaches alternative coping strategies to enable the characters to deal more successfully with their stress.

---

[2] Where pertinent, throughout this manual, the contribution of experts is acknowledged by citing the *person's last name* and the *date of the specific source material*. References for these citations may be found by checking the name and date, listed alphabetically, in the References and Suggested Readings section of this manual on pages 231-232.

The children easily identify with the appealing characters. Without having to admit it, the children can compare themselves to the character's behavior and situation. Due to the program's nonthreatening and nonjudgmental nature, the children are able to use new ideas without feeling pressured. They are able to save face and to get help without feeling disloyal to their family.

Benefits of Use

Using the *Building Trust, Making Friends* group model for at-risk children can benefit your school on a number of levels, including the logistics level, the individual level, and the system level.

The Logistics Level. Logistically, the model provides structure for new and untrained group leaders. The materials contained in the manual provide everything a leader will need to implement a group, including a self-referral group survey form for classroom surveys, a parental consent letter, a screening interview outline, and complete guidelines for each session.

The structure of the group format cuts down considerably on behavior problems during group session. Generally, children (from kindergarten through eighth grade) enjoy participating in these groups and eagerly recommend them to their friends.

The Individual Level. Children who participate in the program have benefited in a variety of ways, including the following: (1) children's behavior in school improved, as evidenced by fewer trips to the office and fewer suspensions; (2) children increased their attachment to school, which has proved to be effective drop-out prevention; (3) middle school students were helped to abstain from alcohol, marijuana, and other drugs; and (3) children integrated concepts taught in the group into other situations. The examples that follow illustrate how children were able to integrate concepts taught in the group into other situations.

Stephen, a fifth-grader, had been sent frequently to the principal's office due to behavior problems, before taking part in a Thomas Barker group for children from divorced or separated families. When, in group, Stephen encountered the basic fact called the 3 Cs (children can't cause, control, or change a parental separation or divorce), he bridled. "That's not true," he said. "At least when I act bad in school, my parents come and talk to each other." By the end of the group's session, however, Stephen had come a long way. "Well, I used to think a child could change a separation," Stephen said. "Now I know that's not true." Stephen was not seen in the principal's office during the entire time the Thomas Barker group met.

Donald, a kindergartner, was placed in a Della the Dinosaur group for children from homes where violence is used to express anger after being referred for his aggressive behavior in school. After hearing how Della sometimes stayed home from school to make sure no one got hurt, Donald said, "Sometimes when my parents fight, they don't send me to school. From now on, I'm going to call my aunt and have her take me to school." This example demonstrates how even the youngest children are able to grasp and integrate the concepts the program presents.

Angela, a first-grader, was referred to a Della the Dinosaur group after Angela's mother reported being physically abused by Angela's father. During group, when Angela learned the basic fact that parents usually love their children even when they are using violent ways to express their anger, she said, "That means when my dad shot through the window at my mom he still loves me."

A sixth-grade girl whose father murdered her eight-year-old brother taught her mother a relaxing technique learned in group ("Breathing Through Your Feet") to help her get through the trial.

After learning the basic fact that children should *wait* until a chemically dependent parent is sober before talking about how they feel, a sixth-grade boy in a Peter the Puppy group told his inebriated father one evening that he wouldn't talk to him until the next day (when the father would be sober).

Sometimes there is a ripple effect from a child's participation in one of the groups, and family members also benefit. One mother entered therapy because her son smiled when she asked him about his group experience. The child wouldn't discuss the group because of confidentiality, but the mother realized that he liked it and was benefiting from it.

The System Level. Since the group model recommends in-service programs for administrators and teachers about issues for children from at-risk families before beginning the groups in the school, the entire system can benefit from using the *Building Trust, Making Friends* group model.

In-servicing raises the awareness and education levels of teachers and administrators about the issues dealt with in the groups (chemical dependence, divorce, family violence). It also helps some who take part to identify for the first time that they are children from such families and to understand some of the problems that they've had or are still having in their own lives. Many who share in the in-service may have friends or relatives who are affected by someone else's chemical dependence, divorce, or violence. Thus, the in-service plants the seeds of recovery for many. Participants may be encouraged to gain further education about these particular issues (chemical dependence, divorce, family violence), to offer informed help to their students who come from chemically dependent, divorced, or violent families, and to seek any professional help they may need themselves.

Chapter 2: Implementing the Group Program

This chapter will help you implement the group program of *Building Trust, Making Friends* in your school, agency, or other counseling setting. The chapter includes information on acquiring administrative support, recruiting and training staff, developing a referral network, screening candidates, and forming and scheduling groups. You will also find information on informed consent, confidentiality, and self-disclosure on the part of group leaders. The chapter will also point out effective means of follow-up on the individual, group, and system level. Finally, it will outline ways you can use the program in guidance counseling and family therapy.

As mentioned earlier, although schools may be able to reach the largest numbers of children, the program may be used in a variety of other settings as well. After deciding where it will best fit in your school's (or agency's) situation, you must undertake the task of getting it started. The first step in doing that is gaining administrative support.

Gaining Administrative Support

You need administrative support. Without it, the program can't exist, let alone prosper. If building administrators aren't aware of the needs and characteristics of at-risk children, you can plan in-services to raise their awareness levels. Principals may feel that they're taking unnecessary risks by supporting groups for at-risk children, especially children from chemically dependent or violent families, and initially may not see any benefits for themselves. If you encounter this sort of resistance from principals, discuss with them the program's low-key profile but very real benefits and its long-term results.

If a school is to support the program, the principal's backing is necessary. If principals establish student support groups as a priority, they will direct teachers to allow children to be removed from the classroom in order to participate. Likewise, principals will also be prepared to answer questions from hostile, resistant, or concerned parents, although such calls are rare.

Offer an in-service to raise awareness levels. Describe how the program will benefit the children, their families, the school, and the community. Describe the common misconceptions that children from at-risk families often have. Explain how displacement communication is used to correct children's misconceptions, while allowing them to remain loyal to their families. Recount how youngsters who learn that they haven't caused, and can't be responsible for fixing, their family's problems will feel better about themselves, will perform better at school, and will be less likely to get into serious trouble either in school or in the community. Explain that learning coping strategies will help children take better care of themselves. Point out how school staffs are helped by their students' developing more positive attitudes about themselves and, thus, about learning. School staff members will feel good about referring students to groups that really work. Good groups will give both administrators and classroom teachers more free time to do their jobs.

If you're blessed with wholehearted administrative approval, it's still a good idea to provide in-service sessions for school personnel to acquaint them with the issues for at-risk children. Design a simple presentation describing the purposes of the program, the role of the group, and the dynamics of the group model, including the group format and progression of themes. The better school staff understand the program, the better will be their acceptance and support.

Staffing and Training

The authorization to provide prevention and intervention services for at-risk children can come from the superintendent or school board, in the form of drop-out prevention, substance abuse prevention, or services to at-risk children. The program will be enhanced if implemented by and with trained personnel. Effective staff may include members of Student Assistance Programs and Core Teams, social workers, psychologists, guidance counselors, chemical dependence counselors, nurses, Drug and Alcohol Resistance Education (DARE) officers, and teachers— all of whom can be trained to lead groups to help at-risk children. Although you'll have to depend on the staffing patterns of your school or agency, keep in mind that the needs of the children will be better met if personnel from various helping professions work together—not engage in territorial battles—to provide services.

The better trained your personnel, the better they'll be able to meet the needs of at-risk children. Training should include the following:

- information about the goals of the entire program
- education on specific issues to be dealt with in the groups (chemical dependence, divorce and separation, or family violence)
- instruction on how to lead groups
- ongoing supervision

One training model might require a three-hour graduate level course on substance abuse, twenty hours of in-service, and ten hours of supervised experience leading groups. Another model might consist of fifteen hours of experiential in-service, during which staff members lead and participate in the program's group sessions together. After this experience, they would be ready to co-lead a group with a certified worker. A third model might have a trainer provide staff development for new group leaders and in-services for school faculty at the beginning of the school year. The trainer then can assist new group leaders in developing referrals and screening potential group members. The trainer also leads a group, with a new leader observing. When the group is repeated during the second half of the school year, the new leader facilitates the group, with the trainer observing and providing supervision.

A fourth model meets the needs of professionals who are implementing this program by themselves. This model combines the expertise of different professionals as group co-leaders: for example, a teacher can co-lead a group with a chemical dependence counselor. The complementarity of skills, training, and experience will again better serve the needs of children.

Finally, you can also check your local resources for facilities that provide training. These may include chemical dependence treatment facilities, state and local health organizations, colleges and universities, and social welfare agencies. You can also find help by turning to a national organization, such as the Johnson Institute, which specializes in training. (See Resources for Help on page 233.)

Developing Referrals

Once you've gained administrative support and have begun training group leaders for the program, begin to develop a list of at-risk children who could benefit from being part of a group. You can build this list by looking to a number of referral sources, including the following:

- school-counseling/social-work case histories
- other school staff
- parents
- schoolchildren themselves
- broader community

School-Counseling/Social-Work Case Histories. Ask school counselors or social workers to recommend potential group members from their case loads.

Other School Staff. Look for referrals from any and all members of the school staff: building administrators, teachers, maintenance personnel, secretaries, DARE officers, Core Teams, school nurses. With the help of your in-services, all school staff members can learn to identify students who may be at-risk. By understanding how the group program operates and the services it provides, staff can refer children appropriately.

Parents. Some referrals will come directly from parents who might disclose during an interview or conference their stress over a family difficulty such as divorce, family violence, or chemical dependence. As leaders become more experienced in facilitating these groups, they gain confidence in asking about the presence of these problems in a family conference or history interview. Many parents will welcome the chance to have their children learn skills for healthy living. Introduce the groups as an educational and preventive service. To allay parents' fears that the groups might be intended to discover pathologies in their families, stress that the groups are clearly designed to educate and inform children, to correct their misconceptions, and to teach coping skills. Describe, too, the instructional process, including the use of the make-believe animal or the fictional student. This will help parents recognize that the group experience will be a positive one for their child, not a negative or judgmental one.

Schoolchildren Themselves. Another referral source is your school's student body. Self-referrals are likely to begin as soon as youngsters become aware of the program and its value. Offer classroom presentations on the various groups you plan to offer. Once the children understand what the groups are about, they'll find it easier to self-refer.

Simply arrange to visit a classroom. Begin your presentation by announcing to the children that you will be offering some groups during the school year, and that you want the children to know about them. To give the children a taste for what happens in group, lead them in a centering exercise (for example, "Breathing Through Your Feet," page 42). Then introduce one of the fictional characters, for example, Thomas Barker, by showing the children the stuffed toy animal. Describe some things Thomas likes to do with his family: play soccer with his dad; play puppy monopoly with his mom and sister. Then go on to describe what happens when his parents tell him they plan to separate: Thomas goes to school but doesn't feel like eating or playing at recess, and almost bursts into tears during science class. Show the children the stuffed toy animal, Mrs. Owl, and explain that she is a helping professional whom Thomas meets. Tell the children that Mrs. Owl teaches Thomas that he didn't cause his parents' separation and can't do anything to change or control it. Explain, too, that Mrs. Owl helps Thomas learn how to deal with his feelings in ways that will help him.

Depending on which groups you'll be offering, repeat the above process by introducing each of the other make-believe animals (Peter the Puppy and Della the Dinosaur) and the stresses in their lives. Be assured that children enjoy meeting the characters represented by the stuffed toy animals.

After your presentation, distribute copies of the Self-referral Group Survey Form (see page 228), and go through the directions on the form with the children. If interested, children can fill out the form, fold it, and hand it in to you. Since the number of self-referrals tends to be high, be sure to tell the children that not everyone may be in a group right away. Assure them, however, that groups will be offered according to time and need.

Broader Community. Sharing information about the group program with parents, professionals, and other concerned adults at a community forum will lead to referrals from the broader community. For example, once therapists and social workers from treatment centers and mental health agencies know about your group program, they will be able to refer some of their clients to it.

When it comes to referrals, the rule of thumb is "the broader the referral network, the better." The broader the referral network, the better the chance at-risk children will be reached and helped.

Screening Candidates

No matter how children are referred for membership in a *Building Trust, Making Friends* group, each candidate should be screened individually before you grant membership. The screening process consists of a brief interview that details demographic factors, the child's adjustment and attitude toward school, and the child's family or living situation. (See the Screening Interview Outline on page 230.) If the child is self-referred, and if you or other group leaders have no knowledge of the child's particular family stress, screening will help gather specific information about it.

During the screening interview, make the child as comfortable as possible, acknowledge loyalty to the family, stress confidentiality, and reassure the child that such questioning will not take place in front of other children. Ask respectfully for specific information about the family stress. Listen carefully to the child's reasons for self-referral, then use your best judgment about whether or not to include the child in the group. For example, a child may refer himself or herself to a group dealing with chemical dependence because his or her parents smoke cigarettes and the child has learned that tobacco contains the drug nicotine. Whether to include this child depends on the child's adjustment and on your sense of the needs and priorities of other group members, the school itself, and the administration.

If you know about the family stress of a particular candidate, and the child is in denial (therefore, generally not self-referred), there's no need to break that denial during the screening interview. Simply help the child see that being part of the group is a way to learn what the fictional characters—who will be introduced in the group—learned about the issues in their families.

If you feel that the child belongs in a group, discuss the group process, including group format and session topics, with the child. Describing the format will prepare the child for what will happen in group and will reassure the child about the safety of the group. Show the child a copy of the Group Rules Contract (see page 168). Explain the rules and tell the child that to be in the group he or she must attend every group session and keep all the rules. If you wish, tell the child that at the first group session all group members will be asked to sign a copy of the Group Rules Contract. This process sets the stage for good behavior during the group sessions.

The prospect of screening every group candidate individually may seem a bit daunting. But such screening isn't just for your sake and the program's sake. It's also a valuable experience for the child. The screening may also serve as a case-finding procedure, during which cases of alcohol and other drug experimentation or sexual or physical abuse may come to light and can be dealt with properly. Naturally, cases of sexual or physical abuse should be reported immediately to appropriate authorities. The screening may reveal that the child needs a group experience regarding another family issue. If such is the case, you can make the appropriate referral.

Acquiring Informed Parental Consent

To ensure a group's integrity and success, you need to acquire consent from the parents whose children are candidates for group membership. Procedures for acquiring parental consent must consider the children's needs, the parents' rights to privacy, the school's desire to help its students, and the provisions of the law so as to avoid any legal action being taken against the school.

The simplest way to get informed consent is to have the school mail a letter to the parents of all prospective group members that clearly but simply:

- describes the program and group process
- encourages parents to allow their child to receive the services the program and group can provide
- informs parents that they must contact the school if they do not want their child to participate (see the Parental Consent Letter on page 229).

If you feel that parents will be resistant, visit with them personally to talk about it. Take along the toy animal you will use in group and share with the parents what it will learn in a fun and nonjudgmental way from Mrs. Owl. Explain the group format and progression of themes. Explain that you're not looking for pathology or problems, but rather are hoping to correct misconceptions and to teach coping skills. Once the program is explained well to parents, few are likely to refuse permission for their child to take part.

There will be times when you, another group leader, or school staff member will identify a particular child who could benefit by participating in a group, but whose parents refuse to allow it. If you've clearly explained the purpose and format of the program to the parents and they still don't want their child involved, there are still two ways you can help the child. First, make sure that the child is present for any in-school presentation about the program, either one you offer as a recruitment tool or one that students themselves might provide (for example, the presentation provided by the optional Session 10). An at-risk child can begin to integrate facts, concepts, and specific skills even when the presentation is brief. Second, you can refer that child to the school counseling services for individual assistance. Some counselors modify this program to use with children individually. Finally, remember, this program is not the only help available to at-risk children.

Forming and Scheduling the Groups

You know from your own experience that the best groups—of any kind—are made up of different individuals with varying temperaments and personalities. The same is true for the groups in this program. To the best of your ability, see to it that groups are a mix of children who are outgoing, shy, talkative, quiet, boys, girls, and so on. However, because of children's developmental differences, you must be careful about mixing children from different grade levels into a single group. It's best not to have a spread larger than one grade level. Kindergarten and first-grade groups can be effective, but kindergarten to second grade is probably too great a spread.

Group size is also determined by the age of group members. Groups of younger children should be smaller, since they require more time, help, and individual attention. To determine group size, follow the guidelines below:

- kindergarten, first, and second grade—four children per group
- third, fourth, and fifth grade—six children per group
- sixth grade and up—seven to eight children per group

For rich group dynamics and useful interactions, eight seems to be the maximum number of participants for the structured groups of this program. When the group size extends beyond eight, the level of individual attention and sharing diminishes. If you find that more children want to participate, offer more groups as it becomes possible to do so.

The location, size, and atmosphere of a group's meeting room are very important in establishing a safe, welcoming space for children to open up and take risks. Generally, classrooms aren't the most satisfactory places for group meetings; they're almost always too large and are filled with too many distractions. Ideally, the meeting room needs to be small, comfortable, and quiet, a place where interruptions and potential distractions are minimal. Privacy is essential so youngsters won't be afraid that others outside the room can see or overhear them. Seating each child at a table will help avoid fidgety behavior and simplify the drawing and writing activities.

Survey your school facility for a good place for group meetings. Obviously, such a space is often at a premium in a school setting, so remember that your most important considerations are privacy, quiet, and regular availability.

Besides matters of space, scheduling must also deal with matters of time. The group sessions are designed to last approximately 45 minutes. Plan to hold them on a weekly basis so that the children have time to integrate the insight and support gained from each session. Weekly sessions are also less likely to interfere with the children's studies and other activities. Try to schedule group meetings for elementary-aged children on the same day, at the same time, and in the same place each week. Although you'll want to make the meeting place and day consistent for middle school groups, you may rotate meeting times so that the children won't miss instruction in the same subject each week. For example, for the first week, schedule the group to meet during the first instructional hour, for the second week, schedule it during the second instructional hour, and so on.

In all matters of scheduling, administrative support is an invaluable aid to help foster teacher cooperation in releasing students from regular classes. Remember, however, that cooperation is a two-way street. Let children and teachers know that students participate in the group on the condition that they make up all missed work. Likewise, give teachers a schedule of group meetings so that they'll know in advance what class a child will miss, won't plan field trips or tests for those times, and can make arrangements for the child to make up missed school work.

Assuring Group Confidentiality

Confidentiality is the cornerstone of safe and supportive groups. To share problems and deep feelings, the children must know that what they say will be kept in confidence. Experts have pointed out that at-risk children are very reluctant to reveal family problems. For example, there are unspoken rules in a chemically dependent family: "Don't talk; don't trust; don't feel" (Black 1981). It's important to realize that the children will not open up if they think that what they share will become common knowledge around school. Group confidentiality, therefore, must be an absolute guarantee.

This program's group model not only guarantees confidentiality but also adds a "plus" to it. Families are accepted and valued in the group, never condemned. The children have opportunities to share feelings and to self-disclose as they choose, all the while remaining loyal to their families. Although they have many opportunities to take an active part in every group session, if they choose to pass, they may, and the group leader respects their decision. Meanwhile, the group leaders provide a corrective experience for the children. By their warm acceptance and nonjudgmental attitudes, they build an atmosphere of trust. Through each session's bibliotherapy, they talk openly about what happens in families. As the children grow more secure, they feel safe to self-disclose and identify and share feelings, which the group leaders help them express in appropriate ways. Remember, however, that self-disclosure is not the goal of the group. Children who never say a word in group can still benefit.

In setting up groups, therefore, take extra care to assure and protect confidentiality. The children must realize that outside of the group sessions they may not discuss who else is in their group or what they say. Children can, however, discuss the facts and information they learn during group. The group leaders must remember their responsibilities as well. Except in cases where the law requires such revelation (for example, where a group leader suspects that a child is being physically or sexually abused), it is inappropriate for a group leader to reveal to others anything a child may share. It's a good idea, therefore, to inform the children of this at the very first session.

But what about teachers in the school? Don't they have a right to know when a child will miss class because of his or her participation in a group? Yes, they do. But isn't this a breach of confidentiality? No, not at all. To help maintain confidentiality, you need only inform teachers that a group is part of the school counseling program and that the children in it are going to learn basic facts about alcohol and other drugs, family violence, or divorce. For even further confidentiality, you might give the groups simple, generic names. For example, call a group for elementary-aged students that focuses on chemical dependence the "Star Group" or a group for middle school students that focuses on family violence the "Moon Group." That way, neither school staff nor anyone else (except specific group members) will know what kind of group a child is in or what the child's specific problem(s) might be. Teachers will only know that one or more of their students are taking part in a group.

Self-disclosing by Leaders

Since the children aren't required or asked to self-disclose, should group leaders self-disclose? If used correctly, self-disclosure can be a useful group technique with children in the fourth grade and up. Even so, leaders should be very cautious and think carefully before self-disclosing. Sharing facts about one's personal life is appropriate only if it's positive role modeling or if it will help illustrate a point effectively. However, leaders should never employ self-disclosure for purposes of eliciting the same from children, nor should they use the group for personal therapy. For example, leaders must not express feelings or share experiences that they haven't adequately resolved or dealt with themselves. From a developmental perspective, self-disclosure is a poor device to use with younger children (grades K-3), who are too egocentric to benefit from such information. Group leaders steer a surer course by focusing on the curriculum and listening to what the children have to say. If you're ever in doubt whether to self-disclose, a good rule of thumb is to trust your doubt and don't.

Role Modeling by Leaders

Although group leaders should make their own decision regarding self-disclosure, the program does ask leaders to share of themselves several times during each group session. Leaders act as role models for important components. Leaders begin the go-arounds for the feelings check-in, the affirmation, and the closing activity of each session. During the feelings check-in, leaders act as role models by sharing appropriate feelings and facts, such as, "I'm glad to see you" or "I'm feeling sad because my dog died." During the affirmation, leaders model what it means to take a positive attitude, choose helpful ways to choose and express anger, or have a repertoire of coping strategies. Overall, it's important to follow the rule of thumb described above. Never share a feeling or issue that you have not dealt with or resolved adequately. Doing so would be poor role modeling.

Following Up Group Participation

Some children who participate in the program's groups will require further services. If, for instance, children have severe behavior problems, it's unlikely that one group experience will enable them to deal much differently or much more effectively with the stress in their lives. Realizing this, be sure to make further help available. That help can come in the form of individual, group, or system follow-up.

Individual Follow-up. A counselor can continue to see the children individually. Follow-up counseling sessions can help them learn to integrate and use in their own lives the concepts and skills the group presented.

Group Follow-up. For children with serious behavior problems, participating in other group experiences can be very beneficial. For example, elementary-aged children who have participated in the group Peter the Puppy Talks About Chemical Dependence in the Family may still have difficulty dealing with or expressing their anger in helpful ways. Such children could benefit from taking part in the group Della the Dinosaur Talks About Violence and Anger Management.

Getting children to participate in another group is usually easy, since they enjoy the familiarity, consistency, and predictability of the group format. In fact, most children who participate in more than one group find that they're old hands at the group exercises, and they like meeting Mrs. Owl again.

Be aware, however, that children should probably not participate in more than one group at a time. Instead, encourage them to spread their participation over one or two years.

System Follow-up. Children with particularly intense behavior problems may require the services of a schoolwide helping plan as follow-up to their participation in a group. Such services can include any or all of the following: (1) individual counseling; (2) successive group experiences; (3) a schoolwide plan for anger management (see the Background and Guidelines section for Session 7 on page 104); (4) participation in a peer counseling program; and (5) frequent consultation between counselor and teachers and other school staff to enable them to help children use coping techniques, such as the centering exercises and anger management. Of course, recognize that you may want or need to refer a child or family for outside therapy.

Using the Program in Guidance Counseling

Guidance counselors and other professionals have found this program's centering exercises, anger management plan, and basic facts very useful not only when working with children in groups but when working with children individually as well. Because the program's concepts, including the basic education about the issues and the correction of children's misconceptions, are clear and easily identifiable, they enhance assessment skills. They also empower counselors in individual counseling with children. Instead of just discussing feelings with the children, counselors can impart information and correct misconceptions. Also, the skills presented in the program are effective techniques that children learn, master, and use.

Guidance counselors who have led program groups have been able to teach centering exercises and anger management plans and use the coping strategy scenarios in classroom guidance. They report that children who have participated in this program's groups are usually actively involved in the classroom discussion, which reveals that children truly do integrate crucial concepts presented by the program (for example, "Divorce is never the child's fault"). Counselors generally report that leading these groups gives them a sense of greater competence, effectiveness, and empowerment.

Using the Program in Family Therapy

The program's group model works not only in schools, mental health facilities, and treatment centers. It also works well in family therapy with families experiencing chemical dependence, divorce, or family violence, or with families in which children exhibit aggressive behavior.

By using the program's format and stories (bibliotherapy), therapists can help family members become aware of and learn the facts about whatever issue has brought them to therapy. They can see the impact the issue has made on the family and their feelings about it. The program can help the family with anger management, coping strategies, setting personal goals, and developing a support system. During group sessions, the helping professional in the stories (bibliotherapy) serves as a role model for parents.

Just as the program corrects misconceptions for children, it also corrects them for parents. For instance, a mother who engaged in long-term conflict with an ex-spouse may come to see that it's important for her children to be friendly with both parents, and she will then lessen her part in the conflict. Or, a father whose spouse is chemically dependent might come to understand that his wife has a disease, that alcohol or another drug is causing the changes in her behavior, and that her problems aren't his fault or his problems. Likewise, parents who express anger by yelling can learn to use—and benefit from—the program's centering exercises and anger management steps. Finally, *all* parents can benefit by learning that feelings should be identified, accepted, and shared in helpful ways.

****

The *Building Trust, Making Friends* program was developed for caring professionals like you who are concerned about at-risk children. It will help you enhance the emotional growth, safety, and self-esteem of these children. It will also give at-risk children the chance to obtain the skills they need to maintain their physical and emotional health and to correct any misconceptions they may have developed. Living healthfully and well is a risky business. All children, especially at-risk children, deserve the chance to take that risk.

PART TWO

Group Guide for
Peter the Puppy
Talks About
Chemical Dependence
in the Family

Chapter 1: Issues Affecting Children from Chemically Dependent Families

The statistics involving children from chemically dependent families are striking. They reinforce the need for groups designed to help at-risk children.

- 28 million children in the United States come from chemically dependent families; 7 to 15 million are under the age of eighteen (National Children of Alcoholics Project 1987).

- Children from chemically dependent families are more likely to develop dependent behaviors in adulthood and have difficulty with intimate relationships (Woititz 1983).

- In an average class of twenty-five students, four to six are probably from chemically dependent homes; an additional four to six students are probably experiencing the effects of the parenting styles of adult children of alcoholics (Ackerman 1983; and Kritsberg 1985).

Since statistics like these reveal that home is where the problem is, children from chemically dependent families require another setting in which to acquire the knowledge, skills, and support they need to deal with the effects of family chemical dependence. The setting in which children spend the majority of their time is school. Thus, school can be an appropriate setting for providing help and support for these children, as well as for offering them some respite from the strong influence exerted by the chemically dependent parent.

The Influence of the Chemically Dependent Parent

As someone who works with children, you're well aware that parents have a major influence on a child's life. Parents' own views, behaviors, traditions, and mores shape the growing child. The influence of a parent who is chemically dependent doesn't diminish, especially in regard to younger children in the family. It continues to shape them, but in very unfavorable ways. In fact, experts consider a parent's abuse of chemicals as a form of psychological maltreatment. A parent's chemical dependence promotes unhealthy patterns of parent-child and family relations, influences the child's social and emotional development, and leaves the child at risk for psychological problems not only in childhood but also later on in adolescence and adulthood. Experts in the field of chemical dependence (Black 1981; Wegscheider 1980; Woititz 1983) have suggested that children of chemically dependent parents experience inconsistencies; receive double-bind messages; hide their feelings; receive incomplete information; feel shame, uncertainty, and mistrust; and experience roles that stifle healthy development and identity.

Still, it's important to recognize that children of chemically dependent parents aren't all affected the same. A number of significant variables determine how a child is affected by parental chemical dependence (Ackerman 1983). These variables include:

1. Use of drugs during pregnancy
2. Child's relationship with the nonchemically dependent parent
3. Degree of marital conflict in the home
4. Age of the child when the problem occurs
5. Sex of the chemically dependent parent
6. Availability of substitute parenting for the child
7. Degree to which the family is organized around the chemical and its importance
8. Presence of violence or illegal behavior
9. Constitutional nature of the child
10. Severity of the disease

Even given these variables, however, children from chemically dependent families still have a higher incidence of emotional, behavioral, and developmental disorders when compared to other youngsters. They have fewer peer relationships, are inclined to have adjustment problems as adolescents, and tend to have higher truancy rates. If children are very young when exposed to a chemically dependent parent, they often have more social and emotional problems in later life than do those children exposed to parental chemical dependence in adolescence. Children are generally more affected if the primary caretaker is chemically dependent, because the person's chemical dependence prevents the consistent parenting necessary for a child's healthy growth and development. Finally, children who have a chemically dependent parent tend to have difficulty trusting others, possess poor self-esteem, and experience difficulty in controlling their impulses. Frequently, such children also exhibit behavior problems, such as excessive fighting, temper tantrums, and impulsive behavior sparked by their hypersensitivity (Woodside 1986; Henderson and Blume 1984).

Clearly, children from chemically dependent families experience acutely and negatively the influence of a chemically dependent parent.

Common Perceptions of Children from Chemically Dependent Families

Children from chemically dependent families tend to share common perceptions about the experience of living in their environment. They feel responsible, directly or indirectly, for their parent's chemical dependence. They equate it with their being "unlovable": "If I weren't so bad, Mommy would love me and wouldn't drink." These children feel hurt by the parent who breaks promises and gives inadequate attention and affection. They feel anger toward the nonchemically dependent parent for not making things right, for allowing them to lose some of the carefree aspects of childhood, and for not protecting them from physical violence or verbal abuse.

Children from chemically dependent families also fear for the well-being of the chemically dependent parent. They're concerned that the parent might get hurt, get sick, or die: "If something happens to you, what will happen to me?" Note that the children's concern is for the health of the parent, not for his or her alcohol or other drug use. Dealing with such concerns, these children often have difficulty concentrating in school.

These children also have intensely mixed emotions. Why? Because that's how the chemically dependent parent acts—mixed up. Typically, the chemically dependent parent is very unpredictable. When sober, he or she may be strict and distant. When under the influence, he or she may be permissive and affectionate. As a result, children not only don't know what to expect from their chemically dependent parent, but also they often don't know what to want or hope for him or her—sobriety or intoxication. If the chemically dependent parent experiences blackouts, this multiplies the confusion children feel. These sad, angry, fearful, and mixed-up children need help.

The Help That Children Need

Children from chemically dependent families are at a higher risk than their peers for developing a wide range of dysfunctional behaviors, including problems with alcohol and other drugs. These children need preventive education and help to affect long-term behavioral change. The goals of prevention and help within the school setting include:

1. To educate children from chemically dependent families about the disease of chemical dependence and their own susceptibility to it

2. To help the children learn how chemical dependence has affected their family life

3. To teach the children strategies to resist using alcohol and other drugs—how to have fun in appropriate ways

4. To give the children an opportunity to identify with healthy adult role models

5. To teach the children how to recognize, accept, and share their feelings and to understand their responses and perceptions about their families

6. To give the children opportunities to master effective coping strategies, including relaxation techniques and anger management

7. To help the children develop a personal resource guide—to know where to go for help

These goals sum up the help that children from chemically dependent families so desperately need. In the school, you can best present these goals, and children can best work to accomplish them, in a group setting.

The Role of the Group

Experience shows that the group process seems to provide the most successful way for children from chemically dependent families to get the help, learn the facts, and develop the skills they need to live healthy lives. Groups serve to reduce the isolation members feel and to offer them needed support and affirmation. Groups are ideal settings in which to present the basic facts about alcohol and other drugs. Supported by others in the group, children can more easily come to learn about the disease model of chemical dependence, which they must understand and accept if they're to grasp how chemical dependence affects their families and themselves.

More than being settings for sharing facts, however, groups are settings that provide opportunities for children to share feelings in a nonjudgmental atmosphere of mutual respect. Groups help children discover that feelings aren't right or wrong—"good" or "bad"—but just *are* (Typpo and Hastings 1984). Groups also give children opportunities to learn from each other's experiences, to accept that they're affected by chemical dependence, and to recognize that asking for what they need is not only okay but also essential and healthy. Groups seek to help youngsters build self-esteem through a better understanding of themselves and their parents and to improve their functioning both in school and in other areas. Through the group process, children can more easily give up the beliefs that they cause, can control, and can cure parental chemical dependence. Possibly, the greatest gift children from chemically dependent families need to receive is the chance to have fun. The group experience can make this opportunity a reality.

Identifying Children from Chemically Dependent Families

You probably have already identified children from chemically dependent families in your community or school who need help. Likewise, you're also probably aware that there are others you've not as yet been able to identify. Remember, you're not alone. Teachers, school administrators, pupil services workers, and others can play an essential role in identifying children from chemically dependent families. As you set about this task, the following list of characteristics (Ackerman 1983) can help. Look for:

1. Signs of physical neglect (poor hygiene, untidy clothing)

2. Behavior suggestive of physical abuse (a child hiding his or her body in PE class or wearing long-sleeved shirts to mask bruising)

3. Marked variation in academic performance and behavior (especially around family pay days or at the end or beginning of the week)

4. Signs of anxiety when a child's security is threatened even slightly (a low grade or missed homework, evoking an exaggerated response from a child)

5. Manifestations of being socially disengaged among peers (a child who is a loner or who is overprotected by a friend)

6. Lagging behind, arriving early, and asking questions about alcohol and other drugs

In addition to these characteristics in children, parents who have poor relationships with school personnel or parents who seem unwilling to comply with school requests or rules may indicate a chemically dependent family.

Children from chemically dependent families live in homes where inconsistency, unpredictability, distrust, denial, and a lack of appropriate parenting are the norm. Trained counselors, social workers, and school psychologists need to address these debilitating family characteristics to help these youngsters become more productive students and ultimately to feel better about themselves.

Understanding Children's Developmental Characteristics

How you help children from chemically dependent families depends on how open they are to your help. This program has been carefully designed to be developmentally appropriate for children in grades K-6. The following developmental characteristics were determining factors in the formation of this group model program.

K-3 Children. Children in the lower elementary grades (ages five to seven) have a high activity level and are generally openly affectionate. By age seven, they have developed a sense of shame, are more careful in their work habits, have lost some of their self-confidence, and require the positive feedback of others. As regards value development, these children experience difficulty distinguishing between actions and consequences. They believe that punishment automatically follows wrongdoing. And they accept the authority of the family without much question. According to Piaget (1928), children between the ages of four and seven are ruled by perception. They believe that what they see *is*. They reach conclusions based on impressions and judgments, not words. For example, if they perceive a cow as purple, they believe all cows are purple. They have a difficult time distinguishing between fantasy and reality. They express their fears and anxieties not through language but through symbolic play. In their play, for example, they may act out scenarios between powerful heroes and villains, or they may act out concerns by playing "school" or dolls.

Grades 3-6. Children in grades 3-6 are judgmental and dramatic. They're concerned with what their parents think of them and stick close to get clues to their parents' reactions to them. By fourth grade, most children accept responsibility for their actions and are able to distinguish between wrongdoing and its underlying motivation. They begin forming close, same-sex friendships. Fifth grade is the high point of childhood. Children experience more self-acceptance, are better at sports, and enjoy organized group activities and secret clubs. Fifth-graders generally enjoy family members and family outings. They perceive parental warnings as genuine expressions of concern and appreciate them, even if they don't always heed them.

In regard to value development, children in grades 3-6 shift from judging actions in terms of their seriousness to judging them in terms of their motivations. These children are particularly influenced by the behavior of parents. For example, when parents model the behaviors they desire from their children, such as not smoking, the children are more likely to follow that behavior. These children are fascinated with how the world works. They're beginning to think logically. They're able to put things into categories and to realize that an item can be in more than one group at a time. For example, they can understand that their mother is also a daughter. They're learning to operate according to rules, such as those found in arithmetic and reading. These children also love board games, sports games, and self-made games that have clearly stated rules.

The session plans detailed in the next chapter were designed with these developmental characteristics in mind.

Chapter 2: Session Plans

Children from chemically dependent families are at great risk to develop chemical dependence themselves or, as they grow into adulthood, to find themselves in marriages to chemically dependent persons (Woititz, 1983). These children are also at greater risk for developing a wide range of dysfunctional behaviors, including other types of dependencies.

Children begin thinking about experimenting with chemicals (alcohol and other drugs) approximately two years before they actually engage in such experiments. Therefore, prevention aimed at children in grades K-6 seems valid and necessary. *Peter the Puppy Talks About Chemical Dependence in the Family* educates and empowers elementary school-aged children from chemically dependent families to make informed choices about their use or nonuse of chemicals. It also helps these at-risk children deal effectively with their feelings and discover the coping skills they need to survive and remain healthy while living as members of a chemically dependent family.

This guide contains eleven group-session plans for facilitating a support group for elementary school-aged children:

Session 1: Peter Talks About Chemical Dependence

Session 2: Peter Talks More About Chemical Dependence

Session 3: Peter Talks About Chemical Dependence in the Family

Session 4: Peter Meets Mrs. Owl

Session 5: Peter Learns About Feelings

Session 6: Peter Talks About Anger

Session 7: Peter Learns to Manage Anger

Session 8: Peter Learns Other Coping Strategies

Session 9: Peter Learns How to Take Care of Himself

Session 10: Group Presentation—Optional

Session 11: Peter Says Goodbye

Each plan begins with the *Objectives* section. This section sets a clear direction for the group session.

The *Session at a Glance* section outlines the session and includes suggested times for each of the plan's components. If you've carefully gone over the plan in advance, this section can serve as a quick reference as you move through the session.

The *Preparation* section, which follows, lists materials needed and gives directions for getting ready for the session. (Note: When directions in this section call for copies of various materials, these may be found in blackline master form in Part Three of this manual, "Support Materials," pages 165-233. One such set of materials is the Basic Facts Worksheets, which will be used in every session. If you wish, when you copy these sheets for the children, you can mount them on construction paper for a special touch, which the children value. Another set of materials is the Basic Facts Posters. These posters make excellent teaching aids when copied and laminated or made into transparencies. You will need to make copies of these posters to use as you present the sessions.)

To assure the best results in leading the sessions, you'll want to find appealing and cuddly stuffed toy animals to portray Peter the Puppy and Mrs. Owl. Securing a stuffed toy puppy is generally no problem, but finding a toy stuffed owl may prove difficult. If you have problems, you can order one from the following address:

Country Critters
217 Neosho
Burlington, KS 66839

Finally, the *Background and Guidelines* section will enrich your understanding of the session's focus and key concepts, as well as guide you through the plan itself.

For the most part, the plan's structure follows the same format for each session and unfolds in three stages. *Beginning the Session* is the first stage and includes a review of group rules, a centering exercise, a feelings check-in (Session 1 substitutes an ice-breaker), and a review of basic facts (starting with Session 2). The second stage, *Exploring the Story*, includes the story, discussion, activity, and basic facts. *Wrapping Up* is the third stage and includes a repetition of a centering exercise, an affirmation, and a closing activity.

This format provides the children with a total experience that is structured as well as welcoming and accepting, instructional as well as creative and enjoyable, challenging as well as affirming and fun. Since the format remains the same for each session, it meets the needs at-risk children have for structure, consistency, predictability, and fun. Each group session is designed to take approximately 45 minutes, but can be shortened or extended to meet local circumstances.

If you are a new group leader, you should follow up each session by filling out a copy of the Process and Progress Form (see page 225). This form enables you to evaluate the session's effectiveness and to track the children's progress. It also serves as a useful tool when training new group leaders. If you are an experienced leader, you may follow up each session by filling out the Progress Notes (see page 226). No matter your experience, it's a good idea to keep some form of notes on each session.

Note: Session 10 is an *optional* session. Its structure varies from the other sessions in that group members will present facts they've learned about chemical dependence to an invited audience. You may or may not choose to involve the children in this session. If you decide to use the session, know that its format and method of presentation will vary from group to group depending on the group members' developmental level and the makeup of the invited audience. For this session to be successful, you should schedule *two meeting times* to present it. Use the first time period as a practice session to help the children decide on the type and content of their presentation, to make all necessary preparations, and to practice their presentation. Use the second time period to conduct the actual session. Again, to guarantee success, plan ahead for Session 10.

These session plans have been carefully crafted and tested. Use them carefully, creatively, and confidently. Everything you need is here.

Session 1: Peter Talks About Chemical Dependence

Objectives

To help the children:

- begin to understand chemical dependence as a disease
- discover that alcohol and other drugs affect how people act, think, feel, and treat others

Session at a Glance

1. Welcome and Group Rules (Group Rules Contract)—4 minutes
2. Centering exercise: "Breathing Through Your Feet"—4 minutes
3. Ice-breaker—6 minutes
4. The Story: meet Peter the Puppy; make Peter the Puppy puppets (Activity Sheet 1); share story—9 minutes
5. Discussion—5 minutes
6. Activity: draw and share picture of someone who's had too much alcohol to drink or who's taken other drugs (Activity Sheet 2)—7 minutes
7. Basic Facts: (Worksheet 1) read aloud; discuss; fill in blanks; read aloud together—2 minutes
8. Centering Exercise: repeat "Breathing Through Your Feet"—3 minutes
9. Affirmation: share something you liked about the group—3 minutes
10. Closing: have a silent wish and squeeze—2 minutes

Preparation

- Choose an appealing and cuddly stuffed toy animal (puppy) to portray Peter the Puppy. The toy will need a dog collar. If it has none, make a simple one from felt or ribbon.

- Make a copy of each of the nineteen Basic Facts Posters (see pages 201-219). If possible, laminate the posters or make transparencies. You'll need Basic Facts Posters 1 and 2 in this session.

- Make a copy of the Group Rules Contract (see page 168), one for each child. To save time at the copy machine, also make each child a copy of each of the eleven Activity Sheets and the nine Basic Facts Worksheets now. (Note: If your group is made up of kindergartners, first-graders, or children from a special education population, you may wish to use copies of the Basic Facts Worksheets with Answers Dotted In.)

- To save time during the session, pre-cut and fold the Peter the Puppy puppets (from Activity Sheet 1) for the children.

- Copy the group rules onto a large sheet of posterboard that you can display in the group meeting space during this and future sessions.

- Have a large manila folder for each child; print the child's name on the folder.

- Include in each child's folder:
    - a 3" x 5" lined index card
    - a pencil
    - a set of crayons that includes the colors red, purple, blue, and yellow
    - a copy of the Group Rules Contract, Activity Sheet 1 ("Peter the Puppy Puppet"), Activity Sheet 2 ("This person has had too much . . . "), and Basic Facts Worksheet 1

- Make a poster to use during the session's Ice-breaker. On newsprint, list the following questions:
    - What is your name?
    - How old are you?
    - What grade are you in?
    - What neighborhood do you live in?
    - Who lives in your house?
    - What's your favorite food?
    - What's your favorite TV show?

- Read through the session plan before meeting.

Background and Guidelines

People who use alcohol or other drugs are not weak, immoral, or bad, but *sick*. Chemical dependence is not a moral failure, but a disease. Like other diseases, chemical dependence has identifiable characteristics: (1) It is obsessive-compulsive: chemically dependent people think about their drug of choice all of the time, and all of their actions revolve around getting the drug. (2) It is primary: the disease causes the chemically dependent person problems in the family, on the job, at school; the disease must be treated before other problems can improve. (3) It is progressive: it gets worse; chemically dependent people lose more and more choice and control over how much of the drug they use. (4) It is chronic: unlike an acute disease like the measles or a cold, chemical dependence never goes away; once people have it, they have it. (5) It is fatal: chemical dependence can kill—through physical illness like cirrhosis of the liver, or through accidents like falls or car crashes. (6) However, it is also treatable.

Fortunately, even though chemically dependent people can't be cured, they can be treated. The goals of treatment are to stop using the drug and to change negative behaviors that people may have developed while using the drug. Chemically dependent people can get better if they admit that they have a problem and decide that they want to get well. Often, chemically dependent people need professional help to get better—out-patient counseling, in-patient hospital stays, and/or self-help groups like those of Alcoholics Anonymous (AA), where people in recovery from chemical dependence work together to help each other get better.

When presenting the disease concept of chemical dependence to the children, be sure to do so nonjudgmentally. Use the same language you would use to describe diseases such as diabetes, cancer, or emphysema. When you deal with how alcohol and other drugs affect the ways people act, think, feel, and treat others, be sure the children understand that chemically dependent people aren't necessarily trying to be mean, but are reacting to, being affected by— or more accurately—suffering from, a terrible disease.

Overall, your task is to empower the children: to help them learn the facts about chemical dependence; to help them recognize and deal with the effects of the disease on their families and themselves; and to help them learn and practice coping strategies so that they can take good care of themselves. This session and those that follow are designed to help you empower the children. It's left to you to add the important human touch that makes for trust, comfort, understanding, cohesiveness, and fun.

Beginning the Session

Group Rules

Welcome the children and have them sit at a table. Explain that this is the Peter the Puppy Group. Everyone in the group will have lots of chances to have fun, learn about chemical dependence, and find new ways to feel better and to take care of themselves.

Pass out the folders. Explain to the children that they will use their folders every time they meet and that everything they need will be in these folders. Ask the children to open their folders and take out a pencil and their copy of the Group Rules Contract. Meanwhile, display the poster you made listing the group rules. Tell the children that like every group—use examples of groups like Scouts, band, and secret clubs—their group has rules. For the group to work well, everyone needs to keep the rules. Even though the children will have encountered these rules in their screening interview, take a moment to go through them now to check for understanding:

1. I will keep what we talk about private. We call this confidentiality.
2. I will stay in my seat.
3. I will keep my hands to myself.
4. I will wait for my turn to talk, and I will listen carefully when others talk.
5. I won't tease or put other people down.
6. I can "pass" during go-arounds.
7. I will come to every group session.
8. I will make up any class work I miss.

Draw attention to the first rule regarding confidentiality. Remind the children that no one will know what they share in group, with one exception. If they share in group that someone is hurting them or touching them inappropriately, you have to report that information to help them stay safe. Once the children understand this and the other rules, have them sign and date their Group Rules Contracts. If group members are kindergartners or first-graders, be ready to offer assistance.

Have the children place their contracts in their folders. Explain that they will be using the folders to hold all their group work, that each week new materials will be added to the folders, and that you will keep the folders safe until the end of the group's sessions when the children can take them home. Tell the children that they can decorate their folders at the beginning of each session, while waiting for the session to begin.

Keep the group rules poster and display it every time the group meets.

Centering Exercise

The first time you lead a centering exercise, it may feel odd to be directing the children to go into a "dark and scary place." Know that the goal of the exercise is not to frighten the children nor to get them *into* a "dark and scary place." Rather, as children from chemically dependent homes, they are already in a dark and scary place. The intent of the exercise is to teach the children some skills to get *out*.

Since most of the children will not have encountered an exercise like this before, give them—and yourself—time to get into it. Begin by inviting the children to relax and by telling them that the name of the exercise is "Breathing Through Your Feet."

> Close your eyes. Imagine that you are all alone in a dark place. It's kind of scary there and hard to breathe. You can get out of that scary, dark place. All you have to know is a secret. I know the secret, and I'll share it with you.
>
> The secret is breathing through your feet!
>
> Imagine that you have tiny holes all over the bottom of your feet. Your shoes are dotted with tiny holes, too. Now, breathe air up through those holes—all the way up to your ankles, right on to your knees, past your waist, right through your stomach, and into your lungs. Hold that air in your lungs. Feel how refreshing it is. Now push the air all the way back down your body—out of your lungs and down through your stomach, past your waist and on to your knees, all the way down to your ankles, and out through your feet.
>
> *(Lead the children through this process five times, for a total of five deep breaths; give directions softly; make sure that the children inhale and exhale evenly and slowly. Finally, conclude the exercise by saying:)*
>
> You've learned the secret of breathing through your feet. This secret can give you power. Whenever you feel scared or find yourself in a scary place, you can use breathing through your feet to get to a safe place in your mind. Imagine that you are in a safe place right now.

(Adapted from *The Stress-Proof Child*, by Saunders and Remsberg, 1984.)

Ice-breaker

Involve the children in an ice-breaker. Have the children get their index cards from their folders. Display the poster you made prior to the session that asks the children to list their name, age, grade, neighborhood where they live, who lives in their house, a favorite food, and a favorite TV show. Have the children write their answers to the questions. Share the information in a go-around. To role model for the children, begin by sharing the information about yourself (you can pass on your age if you wish). Then have each group member share. (Note: For younger children, you may have to ask the questions and get responses orally.)

This safe and nonthreatening activity helps the children feel comfortable about sharing information, and introduces them to the go-around technique.

Exploring the Story

The Story

To get the youngsters ready for the story, show them the cuddly stuffed toy animal (puppy) you acquired and introduce it as Peter the Puppy. Explain that Peter will be with them every time they meet to have fun and to share information with them. Tell the children that each of them will have a chance to hold Peter during their time together, but that they can also make their own Peter the Puppy puppet. Have the youngsters take out the pre-cut and folded Peter the Puppy puppet patterns (Activity Sheet 1) and crayons. Invite the children to draw a face on Peter. Tell them they can make him look any way they want. Some children may make Peter look friendly and happy; others may make him look mean and angry. After the children finish drawing, have them hold up their puppets for everyone to see.

Then, settle the children to hear a story. Have *Peter* tell the following:

> Hi! My name is Peter the Puppy. I want to talk to you about something that's kind of scary, but that's really important. I want to talk to you about alcohol and other drugs. I also want to talk to you about chemical dependence. Chemical dependence is an illness that affects every member of a family.
>
> Alcohol is a kind of drug. It's in beer, in wine, and in liquor. But alcohol is only one kind of drug. There are lots of other kinds. I bet you know what some of them are. Marijuana, heroine, cocaine, and crack are also drugs. So are tranquilizers, nicotine, and caffeine.
>
> Some people can use alcohol or other drugs and then stop. But some people who use alcohol or other drugs develop a disease. This disease is called chemical dependence. People who have chemical dependence can't control how much alcohol or other drugs they use. Taking the drug causes them to lose choice and control over using the drug. It makes them want to take more and more of the drug.

Anyone can get sick with chemical dependence. Grownups can. So can teenagers. People who have chemical dependence aren't bad people, just sick people. They just have the disease of chemical dependence.

Alcohol and other drugs do different things to different people. They can change a lot of things about people. First, alcohol and other drugs can change the way people act. People might not be able to walk straight. They might talk slurred and funny. They might not be able to see too well; things look blurred or fuzzy to them. Second, alcohol and other drugs can change the way people feel. When people feel "down," they may use a drug to make them feel "high." But this feeling wears off, and then the people may feel sick, sad, ashamed, or angry. Third, alcohol and other drugs can change the way people think. People might not make very good decisions about things when they've been using alcohol or other drugs. They may not be able to remember things. They may not be able to pay attention very well.

Finally, people who have chemical dependence might treat you differently when they've been drinking or taking other drugs. They might argue or fight with you or someone else you love. They might ignore you. They might look sad or cry. They might laugh a lot and think everything is funny. They might tell you to do something you know you shouldn't do. When some people use alcohol or other drugs, they might do any of these things, then forget all about them. When that happens, it's called a blackout.

I know about all of this, because someone I love very much is sick with chemical dependence. I'll be telling you more about that later. For now, thanks for letting me talk to you about alcohol and other drugs and the disease of chemical dependence.

Discussion

Lead a discussion to help the children better understand the facts—the key concepts—the story presented. Encourage the children to use their puppets when they speak. To aid the discussion, you may wish to use questions like the following:

- What did Peter the Puppy want to talk to us about today? (Alcohol and other drugs and the disease called chemical dependence.)

- What do you think it means that chemical dependence is a disease? (Look for recognition that chemical dependence is not a moral failure, but a sickness that some people who use alcohol or other drugs can develop. It's an illness just like cancer, diabetes, or emphysema.)

- How do people get sick with the disease of chemical dependence? (Using the drug makes some people lose choice and control over the drug. They just can't say no and want to take more and more of the drug.)

- Who can get sick with chemical dependence? (Anyone.)

- What are some ways alcohol and other drugs can change the way people act? (Unsteady walking; slurred speech; blurred vision.)
- What are some ways alcohol and other drugs can change the way people feel? (Look for answers that reflect the children's awareness that alcohol and other drugs may make people feel "good" for a while, but generally leave people feeling worse. They may feel silly; they may feel angry.)
- What are some ways alcohol and other drugs can change the way people think? (They might not be able to make good decisions; may not be able to remember things.)
- What are some ways people might treat you differently if they're chemically dependent? (Argue and fight with you; ignore you; tell you to do something you shouldn't do.)
- What is it called when a chemically dependent person does different things but can't remember doing them? (A blackout. People who are in a blackout from using alcohol or other drugs act as if they're wide awake, but then later, they can remember nothing about what happened while they were in the blackout.)

Even if you choose not to use the above questions, make sure the discussion underscores these concepts.

As the group discusses, use the go-around technique: go around the group, making sure that each child has an opportunity to add to the discussion. You can pass around Peter the Puppy as the children discuss, giving each child a chance to hold him. Encourage participation, but don't force it. Remember the sixth group rule, which allows a child to pass. Accept all ideas and answers, explaining or clarifying information where necessary to reinforce learning. Afterward, be sure to thank the children for their participation.

Activity

Ask the children to retrieve their copies of Activity Sheet 2 from their folders. Read aloud the text on the top of the sheet: "This person has had too much alcohol to drink or has taken too many other drugs." Have the children use their crayons to draw a picture of someone who has had too much alcohol to drink or who has taken other drugs. The picture should show what they think the person might do or act like. Assure the children that you are looking for their ideas, not "perfect" drawings; stick figures are fine! If a child refuses to draw, give him or her the option to write.

When the children finish, have another go-around. Invite each child to explain his or her drawing to the group. Don't pressure the children to identify the person in their drawings ("my mom" or "my uncle"); the point here is to share ideas, not to reveal specific family problems. If a child should make such a revelation, however, simply comment that Peter also knows someone whom he loves very much that might act like the person the child has depicted. Have the children place their drawings in their folders.

Basic Facts

Tell the children to take out Basic Facts Worksheet 1. Display copies of Basic Facts Posters 1 and 2. Either read aloud the two basic facts yourself, or have the children read them, one at a time.

1. Chemical dependence is a DISEASE.
2. Alcohol and other drugs affect how people ACT, THINK, and FEEL, and how people TREAT you.

Briefly discuss each fact, checking for understanding.

Give the children time to complete the bottom half of the worksheet by filling in the blanks. Then have the group read the facts aloud. Have the children put their worksheets in their folders along with their Peter the Puppy puppets.

Wrapping Up

Centering Exercise

Settle the children and then repeat "Breathing Through Your Feet."

Affirmation

Involve the group in an affirmation. Stand and join in a circle with the children, holding hands. Go around and have each child share something he or she liked about the group. Start the affirmation yourself: "One thing I liked about the group today was…"

Closing

Remain standing in a circle with the children holding hands, and lead the group in the closing activity. You'll use this same activity to end *all* group sessions.

Tell the children that you're going to make a *silent* wish for the child on your right. Then, when you've made the wish, *gently squeeze* the child's hand. The child makes a silent wish for the person on his or her right, then gently squeezes that child's hand, and so on. Continue around the circle until a wish and squeeze come back to you.

Collect the folders. Explain to the group that you will keep the folders and their contents safe until the next group session.

Fill out a copy of the Process and Progress Form (see page 225) or the Progress Notes (see page 226) before leading the next session.

Session 2: Peter Talks More About Chemical Dependence

Objectives

To help the children:

- discover reasons why people use alcohol and other drugs
- learn that people with chemical dependence can't be cured, but they can get better
- recognize that people can do things to feel better without using alcohol or other drugs
- describe one thing they can do to feel better without using alcohol or other drugs

Session at a Glance

1. Group Rules: review—2 minutes
2. Centering Exercise: "The Icicle"—3 minutes
3. Feelings Check-in: color Feeling Wheel—5 minutes
4. Basic Facts Review—3 minutes
5. The Story—9 minutes
6. Discussion—6 minutes
7. Activity: draw a picture of a way to feel better (Activity Sheet 3); discuss drawings—8 minutes
8. Basic Facts: (Worksheet 2) read aloud; discuss; fill in blanks; read aloud together—2 minutes
9. Centering Exercise: repeat "The Icicle"—3 minutes
10. Affirmation: share something that you can choose to do that makes you feel happy—3 minutes
11. Closing: have a silent wish and squeeze—1 minute

Preparation

- Display the posterboard copy of the group rules.
- Have the toy Peter the Puppy and Basic Facts Posters 1 and 2 available.
- Make each child a copy of the Feeling Wheel (see page 169).
- Staple the children's copies of the Group Rules Contract to the inside back cover of their folders.
- Make sure the children's folders contain pencils and crayons (including red, purple, blue, and yellow); then add the following materials to each folder:
  - a copy of the Feeling Wheel
  - a copy of Activity Sheet 3 ("I Feel Better When I. . . .") and Basic Facts Worksheet 2
- Read through the session plan before meeting.

NOTES

Background and Guidelines

Chemical dependence is a disease that follows a predictable, progressive course of symptoms. There are typically four phases in the course of the disease.

In Phase I, *Learning the Mood Swing,* people use drugs for the first time and discover that they like the feeling they get from them.

In Phase II, *Seeking the Mood Swing,* people begin to develop a pattern of use, usually several times a week. Although people may still exercise choice and control over whether or not they take the drug, they begin to make self-imposed rules to schedule their drug use. For example, they may decide not to use before 4:00 p.m., or to use only when they won't have to drive the car.

In Phase III, *Harmful Dependence,* people have less choice and control over whether to use. Getting high becomes more and more important in their lives. They begin to plan time to use alcohol and other drugs and start to hide their use from family and friends.

In Phase IV, *Chemical Dependence,* people use to try to feel normal; to avoid physical and psychological pain; or to be able to function without withdrawal symptoms such as extreme shakiness, nausea and vomiting, paranoia, anxiety, agitation, or weakness. People in Phase IV—chemically dependent people—have lost the ability to choose and control how much of the drug they use. They become obsessed with obtaining the drug. Solitary use and rituals about using both increase. Behavior changes become more exaggerated, and sometimes behavior becomes aggressive and violent.

In the beginning, people generally discover that they like the feeling they experience when they use alcohol or other drugs; they then begin to rely on that feeling (that "high"). By Phase III, people are using to escape from uncomfortable feelings, to avoid responsibilities, and to avoid problems. By Phase IV, people use to try to feel normal and to avoid feeling sick.

Chemically dependent people have a three-layer delusional system consisting of defenses, memory distortions, and enablers. Defenses include: denial ("I don't drink too much"); projection or blaming ("I drink because my wife keeps the house too clean . . . or too dirty." "I use cocaine because my husband works all the time . . . or because my kid is always getting into trouble"); minimizing ("What are you criticizing me for? It's just a tiny bump on the car"); rationalizing ("My drinking is no big deal; I never go to bars"). Chemically dependent people also use lies and excuses to defend their behavior.

The second layer of the delusional system is memory distortions, especially blackouts, repression, and euphoric recall. Blackouts, as mentioned earlier, are chemically induced memory losses: people appear to be alert and conscious, but later remember nothing about what they did or said. Repression is emotionally induced memory loss. Euphoric recall refers to chemically dependent people's remembering the euphoria they felt when high, but forgetting the odd behavior, guilt, shame, and pain.

The third layer in the delusional system of chemically dependent people involves enabling. An enabler is anyone who reacts to a person's chemical dependence by unwittingly protecting the person from experiencing the consequences of his or her use of alcohol or other drugs. Some enablers are provokers: they react out of anger and may engage in verbally and physically abusive behavior and/or in controlling behavior toward the chemically dependent person. Some enablers are rescuers: they react out of guilt and enforce no consequences on the chemically dependent person. Some enablers become victims: they react out of hurt toward the chemically dependent person, soon turn into complainers and martyrs, and become increasingly isolated and withdrawn.

Even though people with chemical dependence can't be cured, they can get better. Treatment often begins only after there is a crack in their delusional system. For instance, enablers may stop their protective behavior; chemically dependent people begin to experience consequences of their chemical use; and if this happens enough, they may admit they have a problem and decide they want to get better.

Treatment has two major goals: abstinence from alcohol or other drugs and changing the negative behaviors that developed during the alcohol or other drug use. Chemically dependent people need to develop positive patterns of behavior—behaviors that make them feel better that don't involve using alcohol or other drugs.

This picture of chemical dependence reveals that it is a *feeling disease*. As such, children from chemically dependent families need to develop ways to cope with their feelings that don't involve alcohol or other drugs. In this group session, you'll help the children discover that they need to develop patterns of behavior to help them feel comfortable, but behaviors that don't involve alcohol or other drugs. Peter models this for the children in the session's story. However, you'll be more effective as a group leader if you're ready to share with the children the variety of behaviors and activities that *you* use to feel better: for example, exercise, listening to music, talking to friends, bubble baths, sports, or playing games. Recognizing that if they feel sad or angry, they can do something to help themselves feel better is crucial for the children in building a foundation for the coping strategies to be learned in later sessions.

Beginning the Session

Group Rules

Welcome the children and begin with a quick review of the group's purpose and rules. Remind the youngsters that they all belong to the Peter the Puppy Group so that they can have fun, learn about chemical dependence, and find out how to feel better and to take better care of themselves. Draw attention to the poster listing the group rules. Distribute the children's folders and have them look at their own copies of the Group Rules Contract. In a go-around, have the children read the rules one at a time.

1. I will keep what we talk about private. We call this confidentiality.
2. I will stay in my seat.
3. I will keep my hands to myself.
4. I will wait for my turn to talk, and I will listen carefully when others talk.
5. I won't tease or put other people down.
6. I can "pass" during go-arounds.
7. I will come to every group session.
8. I will make up any class work I miss.

Check for understanding before moving on.

Centering Exercise

Make certain that the children all are comfortable and quiet. Then lead them in the following centering exercise called "The Icicle":

> Close your eyes. Imagine that you are back in a dark and scary place, sort of like outer space. You know that you can get out of that place by breathing through your feet. Well, I'm going to let you in on another secret that will help you get to a safe place. Pay attention, and I'll tell you exactly what to do. The secret is called the Icicle.
>
> Tighten the muscles in your feet and legs really tight; make your feet and legs as stiff as an icicle. *(Pause.)* Now let that cold and stiff icicle melt. Let it melt drip by drip, into a calm and peaceful puddle. Let your legs get loose and very relaxed, and imagine what they would feel like as part of a puddle. *(Pause.)* Tighten your chest, tummy, and trunk area; make it as stiff as an icicle. *(Pause.)* Now let that icicle melt,

slowly, drip by drip, into a puddle. *(Pause.)* Put your arms straight out in front of you, make fists, and pretend that your arms are icicles. *(Pause.)* Now let those icicles melt; let them drip into a puddle, and imagine what they feel like as they drip. *(Pause.)* Tighten the muscles in your shoulders, neck, and head; tighten them into a stiff, cold icicle. Make them very stiff and tight. *(Pause.)* Now let them relax and melt, slowly, very slowly into a puddle. *(Pause.)*

Take every muscle in your whole body; make them just as stiff and tight as you can. Make your whole self into an icicle. *(Pause.)* Now let yourself melt, from the tip of your toes to the top of your head. Let yourself melt, drip by drip, into a puddle. Let yourself get very loose and relaxed, like smooth water in a puddle. Imagine that your whole body is a calm, quiet, peaceful puddle. *(Pause.)*

You've all just learned another great secret, the Icicle. When you feel scared or frightened, you can let yourself melt—just like an icicle—into a safe, calm, peaceful place.

Feelings Check-in

Do a feelings check-in with the children. Have them take their crayons and Feeling Wheels out of their folders. Direct the children to color in the section on the wheel that shows how they're feeling today. For younger children, read the names of the feelings on the wheel aloud (Angry [red], Scared [purple], Sad [blue], Glad [yellow]). The children can color in more than one feeling, since it's possible to have more than one feeling at a time. Tell the children that if they're having a feeling that is not named on the wheel, they can add a bubble to the outside of the wheel in any color they choose.

When the children finish coloring, have a go-around, beginning with yourself. Invite each child to say his or her name and to show with the wheel how he or she is feeling. Be sure to accept each child's feeling(s) and to affirm each child. Afterwards, tell the children that they will be using this same copy of the Feeling Wheel every time they meet, adding colors at each session. Therefore, make certain the children put the wheels safely in their folders.

Basic Facts Review

To help the children review their last session and the basic facts learned so far, show them Basic Facts Posters 1 and 2:

1. Chemical dependence is a DISEASE.

2. Alcohol and other drugs affect how people ACT, THINK, and FEEL, and how people TREAT you.

In a go-around, ask a student to read the first fact aloud and to explain what it means. If a child has trouble, don't contradict or judge, simply clarify the explanation. Then ask all the children to repeat the fact together. Repeat the process for each fact.

Exploring the Story
The Story

Have the children get comfortable for today's story. Be sure to use the toy Peter and allow *him* to tell the following:

Hello, girls and boys! It's so good to see you again. When we met last time, I talked to you about the disease of chemical dependence. I told you how alcohol and other drugs can change the way people act, think, and feel. Alcohol and other drugs can even change the way a person treats you—even if you love the person a lot, and the person loves you. When that happens, it can be scary.

Well, if you're like me, you probably wonder why people would even use alcohol or other drugs. Today, I'd like to tell you why some people take alcohol and other drugs, even though they make people act so strangely.

Sometimes, when people don't like the way they feel, they drink alcohol or take other drugs to change how they feel. You see, alcohol and other drugs can make people feel better sometimes. But usually, people feel better only for a little while. Then they feel worse.

Sometimes people drink alcohol or use other drugs because their friends are using alcohol or other drugs.

Sometimes people drink alcohol or use other drugs because they want to feel "cool."

When people use alcohol or other drugs a lot, something changes inside their bodies. Pretty soon their bodies need to have the alcohol or other drugs in them just to feel normal. People keep using the drugs so they won't feel sick. But they don't feel good. They can't choose and control the way they use alcohol or other drugs. They are sick with the disease of chemical dependence.

In our first group session, I told you that anyone can get sick with chemical dependence. People who have chemical dependence aren't bad people. They are just sick people. I also want you to know that the sickness or disease of chemical dependence *can't* be cured, like the sickness of a cold. Chemical dependence never goes away. It's like diabetes or emphysema. Once you have it, you always have it.

But, people with chemical dependence <u>*can*</u> *get better.* First, they have to see that they have a problem. Then, they have to decide that they want to get better.

Very often, people with chemical dependence need special help so that they can stop drinking alcohol or taking other drugs. They may need to go to a counselor or a hospital to get that help. They also may go to get help in a special group called AA or Alcoholics Anonymous. In AA, people who are recovering (that means "getting better") from chemical dependence help each other. To get better, chemically dependent people have to do two things. First, they have to stop using alcohol or other drugs. Second they must change the ways they've been acting while they've been using alcohol or other drugs. *(Pause.)*

I've told you a lot about chemical dependence today, especially about the reasons why people use alcohol and other drugs. One of the reasons I'd like you to remember especially is this:

When some people don't like the way they feel, they use alcohol or other drugs to change the way they feel—to make themselves feel better.

When puppies like me and children like you don't like the way we feel, it's important for us to know things that we can do to help ourselves feel better. We need to do these things instead of using alcohol or other drugs.

I'm a puppy who's never used alcohol or other drugs. Some days I wake up feeling happy. But other days, I wake up feeling sad or angry. On those days, I have to choose to do things that make me feel better. Here are some of the things I do to help myself feel better:

1. I talk to the other puppies in the "Just Say No" club at school.
2. I go for a run in the park and chase cats.
3. I play fetch with my dad.
4. I visit my grandma or my uncle, Sam Spaniel.
5. I play with my puppy friends.
6. I'm a pitcher on my Little League team, the New York Barkers.
7. I watch a TV show with my family.
8. I cuddle with my mom while she reads me a story.
9. I draw pictures.
10. I do my work at school so I get a smiley face on my paper.

I bet you'd have a good time doing these things too—except maybe chasing cats. I bet you can think of lots of other things to do that are smart and safe that will help you feel better. Think of some different things you can do that make you feel better. Soon, you can draw what you can do that makes you feel better.

Thanks for letting me talk to you about chemical dependence and feelings. Until we meet again, remember, when people use alcohol or other drugs to make themselves feel better, they're barking up the wrong tree.

Discussion

Lead a discussion to help the children better understand the facts—the key concepts—the story presented. If you wish, let the children use their puppets when they speak, or let them hold Peter the Puppy. As the group discusses, remember to use the go-around technique: go around the group, making sure that each child has an opportunity to add to the discussion. Encourage participation, but don't force it. Remember the sixth group rule, which allows a child to pass. Accept all ideas and answers, explaining or clarifying information where necessary to reinforce learning. To aid the discussion, you may wish to use questions like the following:

- What did Peter the Puppy talk to us about today? (Look for responses that recognize reasons why people use alcohol or other drugs.)

- What are some reasons people use alcohol or other drugs? (They think it will make them feel better; because friends use; to feel cool; because they have the disease of chemical dependence.)

- Do alcohol and other drugs make people feel better? (People may feel better for a little while—they may feel "high"; but when the "high" wears off, they often feel worse.)

- If someone has the disease of chemical dependence, will it ever go away? (No, it's a chronic disease. Chemical dependence can't be cured.)

- Can people with chemical dependence get better? (Yes. But first they have to admit they have a problem and decide they want to get better. Chemically dependent people may need to get help.)

- Where can chemically dependent people go if they want help to get better? (They can go to a counselor or a hospital. They can also get help in a special group called AA, or Alcoholics Anonymous.)

- What two things do chemically dependent people have to do to get better? (Stop using alcohol or other drugs; change the ways they've been acting while they've been using alcohol or other drugs.)

alcohol or other drugs; change the ways they've been acting while they've been using alcohol or other drugs.)

- If you wake up one day in a sad or angry mood and you don't like that feeling, do you have to stay feeling that way all day long? (No. I can choose to do smart and safe things that help me to feel better.)

- What are some things Peter does to help him feel better? (Accept all appropriate responses.)

Even if you choose not to use the above questions, make sure the discussion underscores these concepts.

Activity

Ask the children to retrieve Activity Sheet 3 from their folders. Read aloud the text on the top of the sheet: "I feel better when I. . . ." Remind the children how Peter asked them to think about things they can do that make them feel better. Have the children use their pencils or crayons to draw a picture of what they thought of doing. As in the first group session, assure the children that they need not make "perfect" drawings; stick figures are fine! Likewise, if a child refuses to draw, give him or her the option to write. Children may also draw or write several things.

When the children finish, have another go-around. Invite each child to explain his or her drawing to the group. You might have the children pantomime or "act out" their drawings. Be sure to re-direct gently any inappropriate ideas and to reinforce positive ideas. After the go-around, have the children place their drawings in their folders.

Basic Facts

Tell the children to take out Basic Facts Worksheet 2. Either read aloud the two new basic facts yourself, or have the children read them, one at a time.

3. People with chemical dependence can't be cured, but they can get <u>BETTER</u>.

4. People can do things to feel <u>BETTER</u> without using alcohol or other drugs.

Briefly discuss each fact, checking for understanding.

Give the children time to complete the bottom half of the worksheet by filling in the blanks. Then ask the group to read the facts aloud. Have the children put their worksheets

Wrapping Up

Centering Exercise

Settle the children and repeat "The Icicle."

Affirmation

Involve the group in an affirmation. Stand and join in a circle with the children, holding hands. Go around and have the children share something that makes them feel better or happy. Start the affirmation yourself: "I feel happy when I. . . ."

Closing

Remain standing in a circle with the children, holding hands, and lead the group in the closing activity. Tell the children that you're going to make a *silent* wish for the child on your right. Then, when you've made the wish, *gently squeeze* the child's hand. The child makes a silent wish for the person on his or her right, then gently squeezes that child's hand, and so on. Continue around the circle until a wish and squeeze come back to you.

Collect the folders. Explain to the group that you will keep the folders and their contents safe until the next group session.

Fill out a copy of the Process and Progress Form (see page 225) or the Progress Notes (see page 226) before leading the next session.

Session 3: Peter Talks About Chemical Dependence in the Family

Objectives

To help the children:

- realize that they may not like the way a chemically dependent family member behaves
- identify three behaviors often found in chemically dependent families

Session at a Glance

1. Group Rules: review—1 minute
2. Centering Exercise: "A Safe, Warm Place"—3 minutes
3. Feelings Check-in: color Feeling Wheel—5 minutes
4. Basic Facts Review—4 minutes
5. The Story—6 minutes
6. Discussion—6 minutes
7. Activity: draw a picture of family and color in the feelings (Activity Sheet 4)—11 minutes
8. Basic Facts: (Worksheet 3) read aloud; discuss; fill in blanks; read aloud together—2 minutes
9. Centering Exercise: repeat "A Safe, Warm Place"—3 minutes
10. Affirmation: share something you liked about today's story—3 minutes
11. Closing: have a silent wish and squeeze—1 minute

Preparation

- Display the posterboard copy of the group rules.
- Have the toy Peter the Puppy and Basic Facts Posters 1-4 available.
- Make sure the children's folders contain the Feeling Wheel and pencils and crayons (including red, purple, blue, and yellow); then add the following materials to each folder:
   - a copy of Activity Sheet 4 ("A Feeling Picture of My Family")
   - a copy of Basic Facts Worksheet 3
- Read through the session plan before meeting.

NOTES

Background and Guidelines

As the disease of chemical dependence develops in a family, the behavior of the chemically dependent person begins to revolve more and more around the use of the drug of choice. Then, as drug use increases, the behavior of the chemically dependent person is increasingly—and negatively—affected as well. But the chemically dependent family member is not the only family member affected by the disease. Indeed, all family members are affected by the chemical dependence, and their behavior typically reflects it.

Experts have described characteristic roles that members—spouses and children—of a chemically dependent family regularly adopt. Spouses, for example, typically alter their behavior in response to a husband's or wife's chemical dependence and chemically dependent behavior. On some level spouses might believe either that they've caused the alcohol or other drug use or that they can control or cure it. Thus, they might "try harder" to solve the chemically dependent spouse's problems by: taking over his or her responsibilities; protecting the spouse from the consequences of his or her behavior while intoxicated; or by changing their own behavior, which they think is causing the problems.

For example (using traditional gender roles that could easily be reversed in the 1990s), a wife might make excuses for her husband when he misses work because of a hangover or when he fails to keep promises to the children. Or, a husband might make dinner and do laundry for his wife if she fails to do so because she's intoxicated. In this session's story, Peter the Puppy's mom, Suzy, changes her usual behavior (baking dog biscuits with Peter, walking him to the bus stop, cuddling and reading to him) because of her husband's chemical dependence.

Since spouses of chemically dependent people see themselves as dependent on the user and his or her behavior, they may quickly begin to feel hopeless or powerless. They may see themselves as victims and as failures and as being unable to help themselves. The plight of such spouses is similar to that of a satellite revolving around a planet, stuck in its gravitational pull. Like hapless satellites, many spouses of chemically dependent people are unable to break away, act independently, steer their own course.

If spouses could break away from the pull of the chemically dependent person, they would stop feeling responsible for the person's use and/or behavior, would stop trying to control both, and would stop trying to protect the person. Instead, they would begin to allow the chemically dependent person to experience the consequences of his or her own actions. The spouses could then begin to deal with their own feelings and to set goals for themselves.

Spouses aren't the only family members who alter their behavior in response to a family member's chemical dependence. Children change their behaviors and play roles, too. Experts call these "survival roles." Children take them on to survive in the chemically dependent home and to make life there less painful. The roles typically described for children in a chemically dependent family are *superhero, lost child, scapegoat,* and *mascot*.

Superheroes generally—and mistakenly—believe that if they are only good enough, or perfect enough, their family's problems will be solved. These children try to help out at home, get good grades, be therapists to their parents. They do anything and everything they can to help parents solve their problems. These children live in the misconception that their behavior (if it's good enough) can control or cure parental behavior (get a parent to stop using alcohol or other drugs). Superhero children generally end up feeling like failures, because no matter how good they are, their "perfect" behavior can never be good enough to make a chemically dependent parent stop using or to make the other parent stop hurting over the chemically dependent parent's behavior. Living in their misconception, superheroes may become very rigid and perfectionistic. They may overreact and become unduly upset over the slightest criticism from an authority figure (teacher, coach, clergyperson).

Superheroes are outwardly successful; the family can point to them, feel proud, and say, "We're okay." Superheroes pay a price, however. Generally, they experience feelings of hurt, inadequacy, confusion, guilt, fear, and low self-esteem. They seem to be able to do anything, *except* what they want to do most—make their family well.

Lost children may feel personally responsible for the parental chaos in a chemically dependent home. Rather than trying to control that chaos, however, lost children try becoming invisible. Invisible, they won't be held accountable for parental stress or upset. These children might spend a lot of time by themselves, away from other family members, "lost" in their own worlds. They may become overeaters or underachievers in school, or they may become isolated and withdrawn, seeing themselves as alone, helpless, vulnerable, and powerless. Lost children give a chemically dependent family some relief. Pointing to the quiet, lost child, a family can think that everything's all right in the family. On the inside, lost children feel unimportant, lonely, hurt, abandoned, fearful, and defeated.

Scapegoats tend to be the lightning rods for anger in a family. These children may act out their own anger by fighting or yelling at home or at school. They tend to get themselves in trouble and, in this way, focus attention away from the chemically dependent parent. This further protects the chemically dependent parent from the consequences of his or her behavior. Scapegoats feel hurt and abandoned, angry and rejected, and totally inadequate; they possess little or no self-esteem.

Mascots tend to provide comic relief for the family by acting as family clowns. Like scapegoats, they focus attention away from the problem of the chemically dependent parent. These children generally see themselves as "jokes." Thus, they have low self-esteem and feel frightened, lonely, anxious, inadequate, and unimportant. Mascots may be diagnosed as having an Attention-Deficit Hyperactivity Disorder, or they may have learning disabilities in school.

These survival roles aren't meant to be labels or rigid categories. In fact, children in chemically dependent families may exhibit characteristics of several different roles at the same time; or, over time, they may adopt different roles. For instance, a younger child who acts as a scapegoat may become a superhero after an older sibling (who has played the role) leaves home. Likewise, children from chemically dependent families may exhibit other traits that don't necessarily lend themselves to the roles identified here. These roles are stressed simply to alert you to behaviors *typically* found in chemically dependent homes, behaviors you might find in the members of your group.

As you lead the children through this session, be alert for a rise in their anxiety levels. Peter's story presents the effects of chemical dependence on families in a nonthreatening way. Still, because the story is likely to touch "close to home," expect the children to react. Be ready to validate and tolerate both their feelings and their anxiety. Doing so lays the groundwork for the children to recognize and accept their feelings on their own.

Beginning the Session

Group Rules

Welcome the children, pass out folders, and begin with a quick review of the group rules. Draw attention to the poster listing the group rules. Read the rules aloud, or call on different children to read them one at a time.

1. I will keep what we talk about private. We call this confidentiality.
2. I will stay in my seat.
3. I will keep my hands to myself.
4. I will wait for my turn to talk, and I will listen carefully when others talk.
5. I won't tease or put other people down.
6. I can "pass" during go-arounds.
7. I will come to every group session.
8. I will make up any class work I miss.

Check for understanding before moving on.

Centering Exercise

Lead the group in the following centering exercise called "A Safe, Warm Place."

> Close your eyes. You're back in a dark, cold, and scary place, like an abandoned mine. I'm going to tell you another secret to get you to a warm, safe place.

Imagine or pretend that you're in a place that you like a lot. It's a place where you feel very relaxed and comfortable. This place may be different for each person. It may be a bedroom. It may be a special corner in your house. It may be a secret place in your attic. It may be a place outside that's very beautiful. No matter where it is for you, its a place where you feel very safe and warm and cozy.

Pretend that you're there right now and that those safe and warm and cozy feelings are all around you. You're feeling very relaxed, very warm, very safe, and very cozy and comfortable. When you come back to where you are now, you'll feel very good and ready to work hard.

Feelings Check-in

Do a feelings check-in with the children. Have them take their crayons and Feeling Wheels out of their folders. Direct the children to color in the section on the wheel that shows how they're feeling today. For younger children, read the names of the feelings on the wheel aloud (Angry [red], Scared [purple], Sad [blue], Glad [yellow]). The children can color in more than one feeling, since it's possible to have more than one feeling at a time. Tell the children that if they're having a feeling that is not named on the wheel, they can add a bubble to the outside of the wheel in any color they choose. Also point out that if they need to, the children can re-color a space.

When the children finish coloring, have a go-around, beginning with yourself. Invite each child to say his or her name and to show with the wheel how he or she is feeling. Be sure to accept each child's feeling(s) and to affirm each child. Ask the children to return the wheels to their folders.

Basic Facts Review

To help the children review the basic facts learned so far, show them Basic Facts Posters 1-4:

1. Chemical dependence is a DISEASE.

2. Alcohol and other drugs affect how people ACT, THINK, and FEEL, and how people TREAT you.

3. People with chemical dependence can't be cured, but they can get BETTER.

4. People can do things to feel BETTER without using alcohol or other drugs.

In a go-around, ask a student to read the first fact aloud and to explain what it means. If a child has trouble, don't contradict or judge, simply clarify the explanation. Then ask all the children to repeat the fact together. Repeat the process for each fact.

Exploring the Story

The Story

Have the children get comfortable to hear today's story. Be sure to use the toy Peter and allow *him* to tell the following:

I'd like to tell you what it's like to live in a family where someone has the disease of chemical dependence. I'd like to tell you about *my* family.

My dad's name is Barnaby. I love him a lot. But he has a disease. He has alcoholism. He has chemical dependence.

Sometimes my dad is very nice. Sometimes he plays fetch with me. Sometimes he plays checkers with me. Sometimes he even helps me with my homework. It makes me feel happy when my dad spends time with me.

But other times, my dad acts differently. I don't think he acts very nice then. Sometimes he's busy drinking alcohol. Then he doesn't play fetch with me. Sometimes, he drinks and falls asleep on the couch. Then he doesn't play checkers with me. Sometimes he drinks and helps me with my homework. Then he yells at me and calls me "stupid."

My mom's name is Suzy Spaniel. I love her a lot. Sometimes she bakes my favorite dog biscuits with me. Sometimes she walks with me to the school bus stop. Sometimes I like to cuddle next to her while she reads me a book.

But sometimes, when my dad has been drinking, my mom behaves differently. Sometimes she gets very sad and she cries a lot. She doesn't want to bake dog biscuits then.

Sometimes my mom gets angry and yells at my dad when he has been drinking and stays out late. Sometimes, my dad doesn't go to work the next morning. Then my mom doesn't walk me to the bus stop.

Sometimes my mom cleans up the mess my dad has made after he's been drinking. Then she doesn't take time to cuddle with me and read me stories.

My older brother's name is Milton. He's in the sixth grade. Milton never gets into trouble. He always gets good grades in school. He always does what the teacher tells him to do. He always helps out at home. He takes out the trash, cleans up the toys, and puts our little sister, Crystal, to bed.

Milton never wants to play fetch or checkers with me. And he always tells me what to do. Sometimes I don't like him much. I don't think Milton is much fun.

Crystal is my little sister. She's five years old. She's always off alone in her room, playing with her dumb toy ponies. She pretends they're real and that she's a princess living in a magic kingdom. Crystal never gets into trouble. She isn't much fun, either. She never wants to play with me.

She'd rather play by herself with her dumb toy ponies.

I'm the only one in the family who used to get into trouble. My teacher was always sending me to the principal's office because I'd bite the other puppies. They were always saying something I didn't like, so I'd get mad and bite them.

Sometimes, the principal would suspend me. Then my parents would get very mad and yell at me. Sometimes my dad would get so angry, he'd hit me, especially if he'd been drinking.

Sometimes my parents were fighting when I had to go to school. Then, when I got to school, I didn't feel much like working. So my teacher would fuss at me, and I never got smiley faces on my papers.

At home, I used to fight with Milton and Crystal because they wouldn't play with me. Then my mom would yell at me and send me to my room.

For the longest time, I wondered why I was always getting into trouble. I thought that maybe I was just a bad puppy. I used to think to myself, "If only I could be better, then my family would be better. Dad wouldn't drink so much. Mom wouldn't be angry or sad so much of the time."

That's what I *used* to think. Now, I know that's not true. Boy, am I glad about that.

I used to wonder what "feeling color" each person in my family would be. I would color my dad red, because he's angry so often. I would color my mom blue, because she seems so sad. I would color Milton yellow, because he always seems glad. I would color Crystal purple, because she seems scared. I would color myself red, blue, yellow, and purple, because I have all those feelings.

Maybe you can draw a feeling picture of your family. Bye for now. I'll see you again soon.

Discussion

Lead a discussion to help group members better understand the facts—the key concepts—presented in the story. Help the children identify the variety of behaviors Peter's family exhibited in the story. For instance: Dad drinks too much, yells, falls asleep, and hits; Mom cries, fights with dad, and ignores the children; Milton assumes too much responsibility and doesn't take time for fun; Crystal isolates herself and spends too much time in a pretend world; Peter bites other puppies and gets into trouble in school and at home.

As the group discusses, remember to use the go-around technique: go around the group, making sure that each child has an opportunity to add to the discussion. Encourage participation, but don't force it. Remember the group rule that allows a child to pass. Accept all ideas and answers, explaining or clarifying information where necessary to reinforce learning. To aid the discussion, you may wish to use questions like the following:

- What does Peter like to do with his dad? (Play fetch and checkers, get help with homework, just spend time with him.)

- What disease does Peter's dad (Barnaby) have? (Chemical dependence.)

- How does Barnaby's disease change the way he treats Peter? (It makes him behave differently; he yells at Peter and calls him names; he doesn't play fetch or checkers; he fights with Peter's mom, Suzy.)

- What does Peter like to do with Suzy, his mom? (Bake dog biscuits, walk to the bus stop, cuddle next to her for stories.)

- How does Barnaby's chemical dependence change how Peter's mom behaves? (She gets sad and cries a lot; yells at Barnaby when he stays out late; doesn't take time to do all the things Peter likes because she's taking care of Barnaby.)

- How does Barnaby's chemical dependence make Milton, Peter's older brother, behave? (Milton tries to be perfect and to do everything just right; he gets good grades, behaves well in school; and does chores around the house; he also bosses Peter around and takes very little time for fun.)

- How does Barnaby's chemical dependence make Crystal, Peter's little sister, behave? (Crystal spends most of her time alone in a pretend world.)

- How does Barnaby treat Peter differently when he has been drinking alcohol? (He won't play fetch or checkers; yells at Peter and calls him names.)

- What are some feelings Peter has after his dad yells at him? (Anger, sadness, shame, guilt, hurt.)

- What happened to Peter's behavior in school after his dad yelled at him? (He got into fights, bit the other puppies, got into trouble with the teacher and principal, and got suspended.)

Even if you choose not to use the above questions, make sure the discussion underscores these concepts.

Activity

Ask the children to retrieve their copies of Activity Sheet 4. Have the children use their crayons to draw a picture that shows all their family members. Then ask them to color each member with the color that shows the feeling he or she has most often. Remind them of the colors Peter used to draw his family. Again, assure the children that they need not make "perfect" drawings. However, they should color each person with the appropriate feeling color. If a child refuses to draw, give him or her the option to write.

When the children finish, have another go-around. Invite each child to explain his or her drawing to the group. Afterward, have the children put their drawings in their folders.

Basic Facts

Tell the children to take out Basic Facts Worksheet 3. Either read aloud the new basic fact yourself, or ask a child to read it to the group.

> 5. Children usually <u>LOVE</u> their parents, but since alcohol and other drugs affect how people act, think, feel, and treat you, children may not like how their parent <u>BEHAVES</u> when the parent uses alcohol or other drugs.

Give the children time to complete the bottom half of the worksheet by filling in the blanks. Then have the group read the fact aloud. Briefly discuss, checking for understanding. Then have the children put their worksheets in their folders along with their Peter the Puppy puppets.

Wrapping Up

Centering Exercise

Settle the children and then repeat "A Safe and Warm Place."

Affirmation

Involve the group in an affirmation. Stand and join in a circle with the children, holding hands. Go around and have the children share something that they especially liked about today's story. Start the affirmation yourself: "One thing I liked about today's story. . . ."

Closing

Remain standing in a circle with the children, holding hands, and lead the group in the closing activity. Tell the children that you're going to make a *silent* wish for the child on your right. Then, when you've made the wish, *gently squeeze* the child's hand. The child makes a silent wish for the person on his or her right, then gently squeezes that child's hand, and so on. Continue around the circle until a wish and squeeze come back to you.

Collect the folders. Explain to the group that you will keep the folders and their contents safe until the next group session.

Fill out a copy of the Process and Progress Form (see page 225) or the Progress Notes (see page 226) before leading the next session.

Session 4: Peter Meets Mrs. Owl

Objectives

To help the children:

- realize that chemical dependence is no one's fault
- learn that children don't cause and can't control or cure their parent's chemical dependence (the three Cs)
- discover three things children in chemically dependent families can do to take care of themselves

Session at a Glance

1. Group Rules: review—1 minute
2. Centering Exercise: "Talking to Someone You Trust"—3 minutes
3. Feelings Check-in: color Feeling Wheel—5 minutes
4. Basic Facts Review—5 minutes
5. The Story—8 minutes
6. Discussion—6 minutes
7. Activity: make a Mrs. Owl puppet (Activity Sheet 5)—8 minutes
8. Basic Facts: (Worksheet 4) read aloud; discuss; fill in blanks; read aloud together—2 minutes
9. Centering Exercise: repeat "Talking to Someone You Trust"—3 minutes
10. Affirmation: share something special about yourself—3 minutes
11. Closing: have a silent wish and squeeze—1 minute

Preparation

- Display the posterboard copy of the group rules.

- Find an appealing and cuddly, stuffed toy owl to portray Mrs. Owl. Look for a friendly-looking owl, and add eyeglasses and an inexpensive, imitation pearl necklace.

- Have the toy Peter the Puppy and Basic Facts Posters 1-5 available.

- Have tape or glue sticks available for today's activity.

- Optional: Make a badge to pin on Peter at the end of today's story. Make the badge from a circle of red felt. Add gold rickrack around the edge of the circle. Use rickrack or a marker to put the initial "P" (for Peter) in the circle. (See page 224 for a sample.)

- To save time during the session—especially if group members are kindergartners or first graders—precut the Mrs. Owl puppets (body, beak, and wings) from the copies of Activity Sheet 5. This gives the children more time to color and decorate their work. Make a sample puppet for the children to use as a model.

- Make sure the children's folders contain the Feeling Wheel and pencils and crayons (including red, purple, blue, and yellow); then add the following materials to each folder:

    - a copy of Activity Sheet 5 ("Mrs. Owl Puppet")

    - a copy of Basic Facts Worksheet 4 (two pages)

- Copy the three Cs (from #7 on Basic Facts Worksheet 4) onto a piece of posterboard or newsprint to display during the session. (Note: If you plan to involve the children in Session 10, save this poster for use in the session.)

- Read through the session plan before meeting.

NOTES

Background and Guidelines

Because children don't possess the knowledge and perspective necessary to identify correctly the stresses in their family, they often try to create order out of the chaos that they do see. However, given their developmental levels, they generally do so in "childish," egocentric, and incorrect ways. They develop misconceptions typical of children living in at-risk families. For example, children often believe that their family's problems are their fault, that they've *caused* a parent's chemical dependence: "My mom uses drugs because I fight too much with my sister." Or, some children try to *control* parental chemical dependence. They may attempt to hide or destroy the drugs—liquor, beer, marijuana, or cocaine. This usually results in the parent's becoming angry with the child and possibly physically abusive. Parents then simply get more of the drug. Children may also try to talk a parent into stopping alcohol or other drug use or into seeking help. Unfortunately, although children may believe that they have the power necessary to insist that a parent get help, they don't have such power. Thus, when children are unsuccessful in their controlling efforts, they feel like failures and suffer low self-esteem.

When children believe that they've caused a parent's chemical dependence, they often think that they can *cure* it as well. Children try to effect cures through a variety of means: by getting good grades in school, by doing all the chores around the home, or by finding another way to bring honor to the family (through their efforts in sports, dance, art, and so on). Again, these efforts won't be effective, and again the children will feel like failures.

In this session, the children meet Mrs. Owl, who corrects their misconceptions by teaching them the three Cs: children (1) don't cause, (2) can't control, and (3) can't cure a parent's chemical dependence. This will be new information for many of the children, and they may resist it. While respecting the children's feelings and opinions, you should be ready to help them understand that they really don't have the power to cause, control, or cure a parent's chemical dependence. Point out that not even a spouse of a chemically dependent person has such power. Help the children see that chemical dependence is a disease that can *never* be cured, and that chemically dependent people will get better only if they admit they have a problem and decide that they want to get better.

This session also addresses the *ambivalence* common to most children in chemically dependent families. These children often have intense feelings of both love and anger toward their parents, which, in turn, is often accompanied by feelings of guilt due to their anger. Remember to accept both the positive and the negative feelings the children may express about their parents. Help the children recognize that having such opposite feelings at the same time is confusing, but normal.

Children from chemically dependent families frequently seek to assign *blame* or *fault* for the disease of chemical dependence—either to themselves, to the chemically dependent parent, or to the non-using parent. Again, in an effort to create order out of the chaos around them, children believe that the chemical dependence *has* to be someone's fault. If the children discover that it's not their fault, they generally blame the dependent parent. Therefore, you may have to spend some extra effort in helping the children recognize that chemical dependence is *nobody's* fault. It often helps to use an example that the children can more readily understand.

For example, you might compare chemical dependence to some people's reaction to a medication such as penicillin. Some people develop severe rashes after using penicillin, but it's *not* their fault that their bodies are the kind that react that way. However, it is their responsibility to decide not to use penicillin. In the same way, a chemically dependent person has the kind of body that develops a need for the drug, makes the person lose choice and control over using, and develop the disease of chemical dependence. Help the children understand that a chemically dependent person is no more *at fault* for developing the disease of chemical dependence than is a person at fault whose body is allergic to penicillin. Again, however, the chemically dependent person did make a poor decision to use the drug for the first time.

By teaching the children the three Cs, the session also aims at helping the children deal with the factors of *co-dependence, detachment,* and *empowerment*. It's important that you understand how each of these factors affects the children.

Although the term "co-dependence" is not introduced to the children, the curriculum is designed to help them learn alternatives to co-dependent behavior. A person's behavior may be described as *co-dependent* when (1) a person feels responsible for another's feelings, problems, or behavior; or (2) a person doesn't take action on his or her own behalf, but simply reacts to the behaviors or feelings of another. Co-dependent people may be very controlling of another, or they may worry so much about another that they don't pay attention to themselves, thus never fulfilling their own potential.

In Session 2, the children discovered that they can do some things to take care of themselves. Knowing this is the first step to learning alternatives to co-dependent behavior. As the group progresses, the children will learn that they don't have to depend on someone else for their feelings but can be responsible for themselves, can learn how to deal effectively with feelings, and can choose to do things that they enjoy.

Learning the three Cs also helps the children begin the *detachment* process. This doesn't mean that children cut themselves off from their parents, but that they give up believing that they are responsible for a parent's problem. Children discover that they can love and care for a parent and can express that love and concern without having to control a parent or fix a parent's problem or his or her chemical dependence.

Finally, the three Cs *empower* the children. They help the children begin to turn their focus away from their family's problems and to train it on themselves in positive and healthy ways. The session introduces three steps the children can take to empower themselves. Children from chemically dependent families can:

1. LEARN the facts about alcohol and other drugs.
2. Ask for HELP for themselves.
3. RECOGNIZE, ACCEPT, and SHARE their feelings.

Spend time helping the children commit these empowering steps to memory. Since many children think that such empowerment is a form of selfishness, be ready to help them see the difference between selfishness and self-preservation. For example, you might ask a child to imagine that he or she is one of three people on an island, with only one piece of cake to eat. Eating the whole piece is selfishness; giving it to the other two people and having none yourself is being a martyr; dividing the cake into three pieces and claiming your share is self-preservation.

The children need to realize that self-preservation is a positive activity and means taking care of themselves in age-appropriate ways. The children can't do this if they're engaged in the futile and overwhelming task of trying to fix their parents' problems.

Beginning the Session

Group Rules

Welcome the children, pass out folders, and draw attention to the poster listing the group rules. Read the rules aloud, or have different children read them one at a time.

1. I will keep what we talk about private. We call this confidentiality.
2. I will stay in my seat.
3. I will keep my hands to myself.
4. I will wait for my turn to talk, and I will listen carefully when others talk.
5. I won't tease or put other people down.
6. I can "pass" during go-arounds.
7. I will come to every group session.
8. I will make up any class work I miss.

Check for understanding before moving on.

Centering Exercise

Lead the children in a new centering exercise, "Talking to Someone You Trust."

> Today, we're going to learn another way to get to a safe place. All you have to do is imagine you are talking to someone you trust. Pay attention, and I'll tell you exactly what to do.
>
> Pretend you're talking to someone you trust, someone who is very nice to you, someone who listens to you, cares about the ways you feel, and doesn't tell you to change your feelings. This person could be a mom or a dad, a grandparent, a pet, or even a stuffed toy.
>
> Imagine that you're telling your trusted friend all about your feelings. Your friend listens very carefully. Your friend understands you and cares about you. You feel very safe and secure when you talk to this person. After you talk to this trusted friend, you're feeling a little better. You're feeling a little safer. You look around, and you arrive in a very safe and peaceful place in your mind.

Feelings Check-in

Do a feelings check-in with the children. Have them take their crayons and Feeling Wheels out of their folders. Direct the children to color in the section on the wheel that shows how they're feeling today. For younger children, read the names of the feelings on the wheel aloud (Angry [red], Scared [purple], Sad [blue], Glad [yellow]). The children can color in more than one feeling, since it's possible to have more than one feeling at a time. Tell the children that if they're having a feeling that is not named on the wheel, they can add a bubble to the outside of the wheel in any color they choose. Also point out that if they need to, the children can re-color a space.

When the children finish coloring, have a go-around, beginning with yourself. Invite each child to say his or her name and to show with the wheel how he or she is feeling. Be sure to accept each child's feeling(s) and to affirm each child. Ask the children to return the wheels to their folders.

Basic Facts Review

To help the children review the basic facts learned so far, show them Basic Facts Posters 1-5:

1. Chemical dependence is a DISEASE.

2. Alcohol and other drugs affect how people ACT, THINK, and FEEL, and how people TREAT you.

3. People with chemical dependence can't be cured, but they can get BETTER.

4. People can do things to feel BETTER without using alcohol or other drugs.

5. Children usually LOVE their parents, but since alcohol and other drugs affect how people act, think, feel, and treat you, children may not like how their parent BEHAVES when the parent uses alcohol or other drugs.

In a go-around, ask a student to read the first fact aloud and to explain what it means. If a child has trouble, don't contradict or judge, simply clarify the explanation. Then ask all the children to repeat the fact together. Repeat the process for each fact.

Exploring the Story

The Story

If you were able to get a toy owl, have it—or a Mrs. Owl puppet, made from Activity Sheet 5—ready to introduce to the children during the story to portray Mrs. Owl. Have the children get comfortable to listen to the story. Be sure to use the toy Peter and allow *him* to tell the story.

>One time when I was getting suspended from school, the principal said to me, "I'm worried about you, Peter. You fight all the time. Puppies who fight all the time usually feel very angry. They probably have a good reason to feel angry. But maybe they don't understand why they're feeling that way. I think you should meet Mrs. Owl. She's someone who comes to our school. She talks with students like you about the way they feel."
>
>*(Take a moment to introduce the toy Mrs. Owl or the Mrs. Owl puppet to the children. Then go on with the story.)*
>
>Well, I met Mrs. Owl. At first, I didn't want to say anything to her. Then I got to know her and trust her. Finally, I began to tell her about my family.
>
>First, I told all the good things about my family. Later, I told her some of the other things. I told her about my dad's drinking, my mom's crying, and how my dad and mom would fight sometimes. I told her that I even hid my dad's beer so he couldn't drink it. I told her that I was acting bad and fighting a lot, so that was probably why my dad drank so much. I told her that it was all my fault. I said that things would probably get better if only I could act better.
>
>Mrs. Owl taught me the facts about chemical dependence. The very first thing she said to me was this: "Peter, your dad probably has the disease of chemical dependence. That means that your dad has lost choice and control over how much alcohol he drinks.
>
>"You didn't make your dad have this disease," Mrs. Owl said. "Neither did your mom, your brother, or your sister. Chemical dependence is *no one's* fault. It's not even your dad's fault. No one really knows why people get the disease of chemical dependence."

Listening to Mrs. Owl say all this made me feel worried and glad at the same time. I was worried that my dad had a disease. I felt glad that it wasn't my fault. But I was worried if he would get well. So I asked Mrs. Owl about that.

"If your dad sees that he's sick and decides that he wants to get better," Mrs. Owl said, "he'll get better. But first he'll have to stop drinking alcohol. Then he'll need to learn to change the way he's acting and learn to show his feelings in better ways. Maybe your dad will need some special help to get better, just like people who get sick with other diseases sometimes need special help."

Then Mrs. Owl taught me something really neat, something called the three Cs. *(Have Peter show the group the piece of posterboard or newsprint on which you printed the three Cs prior to the session. Point out each one as Peter presents it to the group.)*

1. Children don't CAUSE a parent to develop chemical dependence.

2. Children can't CONTROL their parent's chemical dependence.

3. Children can't CURE their parent's chemical dependence.

"Peter," said Mrs. Owl, "even if you get into trouble every day at school, you still can't cause your dad to be sick with chemical dependence. Even if you hide all his beer, you can't control his drinking. And even if you become like your brother, Milton, or sister, Crystal, you can't cure him."

When I heard this, I told Mrs. Owl that I still feel pretty angry with my dad when he drinks. I said that I was afraid that maybe I didn't love him any more.

"You probably still love your dad a lot, Peter," said Mrs. Owl. "You just don't like what he's doing. It's okay for you to feel angry about what your dad is doing."

I wanted to know what I could do to help. I mean, if I couldn't cure my dad, what *could* I do?

"You can't take care of your dad, but you can do some things," said Mrs. Owl. "You can do some things to take care of yourself. First, you can LEARN the facts about chemical dependence. Second, you can ASK for help for yourself. And third, you can learn to RECOGNIZE, ACCEPT, and SHARE your feelings."

Mrs. Owl was really cool. She helped me a lot. She became a very trusted friend. She told me that I'm a very special puppy. She gave me a badge that says so.

(If you made a badge for Peter, pin it on him now.)

The next time we meet, I'll tell you some more about Mrs. Owl. Until then, remember, if someone you love has the disease of chemical dependence, it's not your fault! Blaming yourself for it would be a doggone shame.

Discussion

Lead a discussion to help group members better understand the facts—the key concepts—presented in the story. If you wish, let the children use their puppets when they speak or let them hold Peter the Puppy or Mrs. Owl. As the group discusses, remember to use the go-around technique: go around the group, making sure that each child has an opportunity to add to the discussion. Remember the group rule that allows a child to pass. Accept all ideas and answers, explaining or clarifying information where necessary to reinforce learning. To aid the discussion, you may use questions like the following:

- Who is Mrs. Owl? (A lady who comes to school to talk to children about how they feel.)

- What were some of the things Mrs. Owl taught Peter about chemical dependence? (It's a disease that makes a person lose choice and control over how much alcohol or other drugs he or she uses; chemical dependence is no one's fault.)

- What do you think Mrs. Owl meant when she said, "Chemical dependence is *no one's* fault"? (No one can cause someone to develop the disease of chemical dependence, even if a chemically dependent person blames you for it. A chemically dependent person may have made a poor decision when he or she started using alcohol or other drugs, but it's not even his or her fault that the person developed the disease of chemical dependence.)

- Could Peter—or his mom, sister, or brother—have caused Peter's dad to get the disease of chemical dependence? (No.)

- What are the three Cs? (Children don't CAUSE a parent to develop chemical dependence. Children can't CONTROL their parent's chemical dependence. Children can't CURE their parent's chemical dependence.)

(Take time here to help the children learn the three Cs by heart. Use the poster you made prior to the session. Read each of the three Cs and have the children repeat after you.)

- Why would children think they could *cause* a parent to have chemical dependence? (They may think a parent uses alcohol or other drugs because they misbehave in school; get poor grades; don't listen well to parents; or fight with sisters and brothers.)

- Can any of these things cause a parent to get chemical dependence? (No.)

- What are some ways children might try to *control* a parent's chemical dependence? (By destroying or hiding a parent's alcohol or other drugs; by telling a parent to stop drinking or using drugs; by urging a parent to go to the hospital for help.)

- What might happen if a child tries to do any of these things? (The chemically dependent parent might become angry at the child; the parent will probably go out to get more of the alcohol or other drug; the parent probably won't stop using or go to get help.)

- What might children try to do to *cure* a parent's chemical dependence? (They may try to be perfect and get good grades in school, like Milton; try never to cause any trouble, like Crystal.)

- Will any of these things ever cure a parent's disease? (No.)
- Since children can't cure their parent's chemical dependence, what can they do for themselves? (Learn the facts about chemical dependence; ask for help for themselves; learn to recognize, accept, and share their feelings.)

Even if you choose not to use the above questions, make sure the discussion underscores these concepts.

Activity

Ask the children to retrieve their precut Mrs. Owl puppets (from Activity Sheet 5). Have glue sticks or tape available. Display the sample Mrs. Owl puppet you made prior to the session. Invite the youngsters to color Mrs. Owl in any way they like. Then show them how to use glue or tape to complete their puppets. If you're working with younger children, you may need to offer help. When the children finish, ask them to set aside their puppets for a moment.

Basic Facts

Tell the children to take out Basic Facts Worksheet 4. Either read aloud the new basic facts yourself, or have the children read them one at a time.

6. When someone is chemically dependent, it's nobody's FAULT.

7. The three **Cs** are:
    1. Children don't CAUSE a parent to develop chemical dependence.
    2. Children can't CONTROL their parent's chemical dependence.
    3. Children can't CURE their parent's chemical dependence.

8. Children from chemically dependent families can:
    1. LEARN the facts about alcohol and other drugs.
    2. Ask for HELP for themselves.
    3. RECOGNIZE, ACCEPT, and SHARE their feelings.

Briefly discuss each fact, checking for understanding.

Give the children time to complete the bottom half of the worksheet by filling in the blanks. Then have the group read the facts aloud. Ask the children to put their worksheets in their folders.

Wrapping Up

Centering Exercise

Settle the children and then repeat "Talking to Someone You Trust." If you wish, let the children hold their Mrs. Owl puppets as their "trusted friend." Afterward, tell the children that they may either take Mrs. Owl home today to be a trusted friend, or they may leave her in their folders.

Affirmation

Involve the group in an affirmation. Stand and join in a circle with the children, holding hands. Go around and have the children share something about themselves that they think is special. Begin the affirmation yourself: "I am special because...."

Closing

Remain standing in a circle with the children, holding hands, and lead the group in the closing activity. Tell the children that you're going to make a *silent* wish for the child on your right. Then, when you've made the wish, *gently squeeze* the child's hand. The child makes a silent wish for the person on his or her right, then gently squeezes that child's hand, and so on. Continue around the circle until a wish and squeeze come back to you.

Collect the folders. Fill out a copy of the Process and Progress Form (see page 225) or the Progress Notes (see page 226) before leading the next session.

Session 5: Peter Learns About Feelings

Objectives

To help the children:

- identify four different feelings
- discover that feelings aren't good or bad, or right or wrong; they just *are*
- learn what it means to recognize, accept, and share feelings

Session at a Glance

1. Group Rules: review—1 minute
2. Centering Exercise: "The Clouds"—3 minutes
3. Feelings Check-in: color Feeling Wheel—5 minutes
4. Basic Facts Review—5 minutes
5. The Story—6 minutes
6. Discussion—6 minutes
7. Activity: color in feelings (Activity Sheet 6)—9 minutes
8. Basic Facts: (Worksheet 5) read aloud; discuss; fill in blanks; read aloud together—3 minutes
9. Centering Exercise: repeat "The Clouds"—3 minutes
10. Affirmation: share something that makes you feel happy—3 minutes
11. Closing: have a silent wish and squeeze—1 minute

Preparation

- Display the posterboard copy of the group rules.
- Have the toy Peter the Puppy, the toy Mrs. Owl or Mrs. Owl puppet, and Basic Facts Posters 1-8 available.
- Make sure the children's folders contain the Feeling Wheel and pencils and crayons (including red, purple, blue, and yellow); then add the following materials to each folder:
    - a copy of Activity Sheet 6 ("Feelings")
    - a copy of Basic Facts Worksheet 5
- Read through the session plan before meeting.

NOTES

Background and Guidelines

In their last session, the children discovered three things children in chemically dependent families can do—three steps they can take—to take care of themselves: (1) learn the facts about chemical dependence; (2) ask for help for themselves; (3) recognize, accept, and share their feelings. This session helps the children learn what recognizing, accepting, and sharing feelings means.

Many people minimize or deny their feelings, or pretend they are without feelings. Many people fear feelings. They may fear pain, being overwhelmed by their feelings, or losing control of themselves. These people may try to swallow their feelings. However, no matter how hard people try to hold them down, the feelings don't go away Sometimes they show themselves in physical aches and pains (somatizing). Other times they get expressed through external acting out (fighting, disrespect, delinquent behavior). Or, they may be expressed internally (depression, suicidal thoughts).

Many people who try to avoid feelings do so thinking that feelings are permanent. They are not. Unfortunately, many people often behave or take action based on this misconception. For instance, very depressed people may attempt suicide because they believe that their depression is a permanent condition. Feelings, however, are temporary and fleeting. Children need to understand that they can learn to tolerate uncomfortable feelings until they pass or until they can do something to make themselves feel better.

In this session, the children learn that feelings are natural and normal, and that they shouldn't be judgmental about the way they feel. At the same time, the children also begin to understand that they can be responsible for the way they express their feelings. They can use some feelings to work for them; they can express other feelings so they can let them go. Session 6 will develop these concepts even further.

As you lead the children through this session, keep in mind that a particular emotion can be said to possess three components: feeling, thinking, and behavior. Children can't control the feelings they get, but they are able to control their behavior. Sometimes, looking at their thinking can help children control behavior. For example, children may feel sad because their parents are sad. Seeing the sadness of their parents, children think (or "self-talk"): "I can't be happy if my parents are sad." Their behavior might be crying or withdrawing into inactivity. But children can examine their thinking and change their self-talk: "I can't be responsible for the way my parents feel. My parents feel sad, but *I* don't have to feel sad. I'm different from my parents. I'm responsible for *my* feelings. If I *do* feel sad, I can choose to do something to help me feel better (play a game, read, listen to music, exercise)."

As group leader, you should be ready for some intense feelings from the children, which are normal reactions from children living with trauma. For example, it's not unlikely to hear a child from a chemically dependent family vehemently say, "I hate my daddy! He hits me every day, even when I didn't do anything wrong. I wish he were dead!" If you hear statements like this, don't succumb to the temptation to tell children *not* to feel a certain way. Doing so discounts and invalidates the children's feelings. Never tell the children not to feel what they say they're feeling. Instead, help the children see that they need to identify, validate, accept, tolerate, and express their anger in helpful ways.

For example, if a child who's been hit by a parent speaks of feeling angry in group, identify the feeling: "I can tell you're feeling angry"; validate it: "Most children feel angry like you do when their parents hit them"; tolerate it: "Tell me more about how angry you feel when your daddy hits you;" and encourage the child to express his or her anger in a helpful way: "Some kids draw a picture of how angry they feel or they play with some clay and express their anger by squeezing the clay over and over." Leading children through this process helps children let go of their anger.

This session simplifies the process (identification, validation, acceptance, toleration, and expression) for the children. They learn that instead of swallowing their feelings, it's better for them to recognize, accept, and share their feelings with someone they trust. With your help, the children can discover (1) words to recognize and identify (name) their feelings; (2) how to accept their feelings (remember, feelings aren't right or wrong—they just are); and (3) appropriate ways to express their feelings.

Beginning the Session

Group Rules

Welcome the children, pass out folders, and begin with a quick review of the group rules. Draw attention to the poster listing the group rules. Read the rules aloud, or call on different children to read them one at a time.

1. I will keep what we talk about private.
   We call this confidentiality.
2. I will stay in my seat.
3. I will keep my hands to myself.
4. I will wait for my turn to talk,
   and I will listen carefully when others talk.
5. I won't tease or put other people down.
6. I can "pass" during go-arounds.
7. I will come to every group session.
8. I will make up any class work I miss.

Check for understanding before moving on.

Centering Exercise

Lead the children in a new centering exercise, "The Clouds."

Close your eyes and relax. This centering exercise can help you learn how to handle your feelings.

You're in the middle of a large playground. It's a wonderful place, in the middle of a big, open field. There's lots of space to play and run around. After playing for a while, you lie down on the soft, green grass. You're feeling happy.

Look up and see a blue sky dotted with clouds. Pretend that you're the sky and that those clouds are like the feelings you have. Watch the clouds move across the sky. See how they come and go. They're like your feelings. They come and go, too, like clouds in the sky.

Look what's coming now. It's a big storm cloud, filling the sky. It's filled with thunder and lightning. Your feeling of anger is like that cloud. It's a loud, crashing, shocking, scary feeling! But look! That big storm cloud is going away. The sun begins to shine, and the sky is bright blue again.

Slowly, a rain cloud approaches. Soon it's raining—first just a few drops; then it rains harder. The sky looks gray and sad. Before you know it, a heavy, steady rain is falling. You remember how you felt when your best friend moved away, or when a pet died, or maybe even when a grandma or grandpa died. You felt sad like the clouds in a rainy sky. But the rain cloud doesn't last forever, just like sadness doesn't last forever. Soon the rain stops. The sky turns from gray to blue once again.

Now imagine that you're back home. You're in your bedroom. It's the middle of the night. You look up to the ceiling and a magic window opens up so you can see the night sky. The wind is blowing. The moon is shining. Lots of clouds fill the sky. These are scary clouds. They make strange and frightening shapes against the moonlight. These clouds are like your feelings of being scared or worried or afraid. But listen. The wind is dying down. The scary clouds are going away. Look! The moon is shining. You fall back asleep.

Now you're back on the playground. The sky above is blue and beautiful. The clouds in the sky are white and fluffy, like big marshmallows. They go dancing across the sky. These clouds are like feelings of happiness, cheerfulness, or even love. They make you feel warm and happy inside. They put a smile on your face. But these clouds drift away, too. Soon, the sky is blue and clear once more.

Your feelings are like clouds in the sky. They come, just like clouds do. Sooner or later, they go away, just like the clouds.

Feelings Check-in

Do a feelings check-in with the children. Have them take their crayons and Feeling Wheels out of their folders. Direct the children to color in the section on the wheel that shows how they're feeling today. For younger children, read the names of the feelings on the wheel aloud (Angry [red], Scared [purple], Sad [blue], Glad [yellow]). The children can color in more than one feeling, since it's possible to have more than one feeling at a time. Tell the children that if they're having a feeling that is not named on the wheel, they can add a bubble to the outside of the wheel in any color they choose. Also point out that if they need to, the children can re-color a space.

When the children finish coloring, have a go-around, beginning with yourself. Invite each child to say his or her name and to show with the wheel how he or she is feeling. Be sure to accept each child's feeling(s) and to affirm each child. Ask the children to return the wheels to their folders.

Basic Facts Review

To help the children review the basic facts learned so far, show them Basic Facts Posters 1-8:

1. Chemical dependence is a DISEASE.
2. Alcohol and other drugs affect how people ACT, THINK, and FEEL, and how people TREAT you.
3. People with chemical dependence can't be cured, but they can get BETTER.
4. People can do things to feel BETTER without using alcohol or other drugs.
5. Children usually LOVE their parents, but since alcohol and other drugs affect how people act, think, feel, and treat you, children may not like how their parent BEHAVES when the parent uses alcohol or other drugs.
6. When someone is chemically dependent, it's nobody's FAULT.
7. The three **Cs** are:
    1. Children don't CAUSE a parent to develop chemical dependence.
    2. Children can't CONTROL their parent's chemical dependence.
    3. Children can't CURE their parent's chemical dependence.
8. Children from chemically dependent families can:
    1. LEARN the facts about alcohol and other drugs.
    2. Ask for HELP for themselves.
    3. RECOGNIZE, ACCEPT, and SHARE their feelings.

In a go-around, ask a student to read the first fact aloud and to explain what it means. If a child has trouble, don't contradict or judge, simply clarify the explanation. Then ask all the children to repeat the fact together. Repeat the process for each fact.

Exploring the Story

The Story

Have the children get comfortable to listen to today's story. Invite them to hold onto their Peter the Puppy and Mrs. Owl puppets as they listen. Use the Peter the Puppy and Mrs. Owl toys to tell the story.

Hi, kids. The last time I saw you, I told you about how Mrs. Owl helped me learn the three **Cs**. She also told me about three steps I can take for myself. I can:

1. LEARN the facts about alcohol and other drugs.

2. Ask for HELP for myself.

3. Learn to RECOGNIZE, ACCEPT, and SHARE my feelings.

Mrs. Owl taught me that it's okay to ask for help, and that one way to get help is to have someone help me learn about feelings. You see, I was having a whole bunch of feelings about my family, but I didn't really know what they were. Mrs. Owl helped me *recognize* my feelings, *accept* my feelings, and *share* my feelings.

"Now, Peter," she said, "recognizing feelings just means being able to name them. Accepting feelings just means telling yourself that it's okay to have them—no matter what they are. And sharing feelings just means telling someone you trust how you feel."

"Feelings aren't good or bad," said Mrs. Owl. "Feelings just ARE."

Mrs. Owl helped me recognize and accept the different kinds of feelings I was having about my family. Here are some of those feelings:

When my parents fought about my dad's drinking alcohol, I felt SCARED.

When my mom cried because my dad drank so much, I felt WORRIED.

When my dad was drunk and yelled at me, I felt UPSET.

When my dad called me "stupid," I felt HURT.

When my dad wouldn't play fetch with me and fell asleep on the couch because he drank too much, I felt ANGRY.

When my dad didn't drink and we watched TV together, I felt HAPPY.

Mrs. Owl said, "Peter, if you don't learn to share your feelings with someone you trust, it's like swallowing your feelings whole! It's like hiding them inside, pretending that you don't have them. Pretty soon, you'll be all filled up with your feelings. You might feel like your puppy collar is getting tighter and tighter. You might even feel sick. You might feel sad all the time because of the mixed up feelings inside. Or, you might even 'explode,' get really angry, and let your feelings out by biting other puppies."

Then Mrs. Owl taught me a neat trick. She told me to imagine that I was in a dark and scary place filled with uncomfortable feelings. Then she taught me how to get out of that place, by imagining that I was talking to someone I trust, like my mom, or my pet goldfish, or my favorite toy boy, Harvey. So I tried it. I imagined I was talking to my favorite toy boy. It worked. It was easy talking to Harvey. I told him all my feelings. Then I felt like I was in a safe place. Later I was even able to tell my feelings to Mrs. Owl.

I hope that soon you'll be able to recognize, accept, and share your feelings with someone you trust, too. Take it from me, Peter the Puppy, it works—no bones about it!

Discussion

Lead a discussion to help group members better understand the facts—the key concepts—presented in the story. Let the children use their puppets when they speak; let them hold Peter the Puppy or Mrs. Owl as they share. As the group discusses, remember to go around, making sure that each child has an opportunity to add to the discussion. Encourage participation, but don't force it. Remember the group rule that allows a child to pass. Accept all ideas and answers, explaining or clarifying information where necessary to reinforce learning. To aid the discussion, you may use questions like the following:

- What does it mean to *recognize* feelings? (To know what you're feeling and to name the feeling.)

- What are the names of some feelings that Peter had? (Scared, worried, upset, hurt, angry, happy.)

- What does it mean to *accept* feelings? (To tell yourself that no matter what you're feeling, it's okay to have that feeling.)

- What does it mean to swallow a feeling? (To pretend that you don't have it; to hide it inside.)

- What happens when you swallow feelings? (You might feel sick or sad or "explode" and hurt someone.)

- What do you think are some ways we could share feelings? (Look for answers like the following: talk to someone; write a story; draw a picture.)
- Are some feelings "good" and some feelings "bad"? (No. Feelings simply *are*.)

Even if you choose not to use the above questions, make sure the discussion underscores these concepts.

Activity

Ask the children to retrieve their copies of Activity Sheet 6. Make sure that the children still have their crayons (purple, yellow, red, and blue). This activity gives the children an opportunity to share their feelings in a nonthreatening way. If the group members are older children, have them complete the entire sheet on their own. However, process the eight items listed on the sheet, one at a time. For instance, have a go-around where each child can share how he or she feels when told to go to bed. After everyone who wants to has shared, move on to the next item.

If group members are younger children, it's best if you read each item, being sure to mention the color and corresponding feeling the children may choose; have the children color the item; then process the item in a go-around before moving on to the next item.

Be ready to deal with any feelings that may surface among the children. Validate and tolerate all feelings. Remind the children that it's perfectly okay to have *any* feeling. Also remind them that feelings—all feelings—are passing, just like clouds. They change from day to day. The children can place Activity Sheet 6 back in their folders.

Basic Facts

Tell the children to take out Basic Facts Worksheet 5. Either read aloud the two new basic facts yourself, or have the children read them, one at a time.

9. Feelings aren't good or bad, or right or wrong; they just <u>ARE</u>.
10. Instead of swallowing feelings, it's better to <u>RECOGNIZE</u> them, <u>ACCEPT</u> them, and <u>SHARE</u> them with someone you trust.

Briefly discuss each fact, checking for understanding.

Give the children time to complete the bottom half of the worksheet by filling in the blanks. Then have the group read the facts aloud. Have the children put their worksheets in their folders, along with their puppets.

Wrapping Up

Centering Exercise

Settle the children and then repeat "The Clouds."

Affirmation

Involve the group in an affirmation. Stand and join in a circle with the children, holding hands. Go around and have the children share something that makes them feel happy. Begin the affirmation yourself: "I feel happy when...."

Closing

Remain standing in a circle with the children, holding hands, and lead the group in the closing activity. Tell the children that you're going to make a *silent* wish for the child on your right. Then, when you've made the wish, gently squeeze the child's hand. The child makes a silent wish for the person on his or her right, then *gently squeezes* that child's hand, and so on. Continue around the circle until a wish and squeeze come back to you.

Collect the folders. Fill out a copy of the Process and Progress Form (see page 225) or the Progress Notes (see page 226) before leading the next session.

Session 6: Peter Talks About Anger

Objectives

To help the children:

- identify two ways to make their anger work for them
- discover what coping means
- learn three things they can do about problems they can't change

Session at a Glance

1. Group Rules: review—1 minute
2. Centering Exercise:"The Space Shuttle"—3 minutes
3. Feelings Check-in: color Feeling Wheel—5 minutes
4. Basic Facts Review—6 minutes
5. The Story—7 minutes
6. Discussion—7 minutes
7. Activity: draw a way to use anger to work for you by giving you power to make changes in yourself (Activity Sheet 7)—7 minutes
8. Basic Facts: (Worksheet 6) read aloud; discuss; fill in blanks; read aloud together—2 minutes
9. Centering Exercise: repeat "The Space Shuttle"—3 minutes
10. Affirmation: share one way you can make your anger work for you by making changes in yourself—3 minutes
11. Closing: have a silent wish and squeeze—1 minute

Preparation

- Display the posterboard copy of the group rules.
- Have the toy Peter the Puppy, the toy Mrs. Owl, and Basic Facts Posters 1-10 available.
- Make sure the children's folders contain the Feeling Wheel and pencils and crayons (including red, purple, blue, and yellow); then add the following materials to each folder:
  - a copy of Activity Sheet 7 ("Anger at Work")
  - a copy of Basic Facts Worksheet 6
- Read through the session plan before meeting.

NOTES

Background and Guidelines

Anger is a common emotion. The average person feels anger twelve to fourteen times a day. Yet, most people have grown up in homes where they were taught that anger is an unacceptable feeling: "Good and decent people don't get angry." In chemically dependent homes, most uncomfortable feelings—like anger—are not tolerated. Most children from these homes have had no role models to show them how to express anger appropriately. Thus, as group leader, your ability to show that anger *is* acceptable and that there *are* ways not only to *express* it appropriately but to *use* it becomes crucial for the children in your group.

In this session, the children discover that their anger is a legitimate emotion. They begin to see anger as an energy or power that they can use positively to work for them. They discover that they can use their anger to solve problems or to make powerful changes in themselves. As group leader, you can help the children by giving specific examples. To a child who has been fighting on the school bus, you might say: "If you're angry because other kids hit you on the bus, you *can't* use your anger to change *them*. But you *can* use your anger to change *yourself* and to learn how to control yourself so you don't hit back. You can use your anger to give you power to tell those kids, in a strong voice, 'Keep your hands to yourself!'" To a kindergartner whose parents fight and don't send him or her to school, you can say: "You can use your anger to take care of yourself. You can dress, eat, and go to the bus stop by yourself. Or, you can ask a relative to take you to school. You can use your anger to take care of yourself. You don't have to feel powerless and helpless."

In light of the three Cs, the children also learn there are things that make them feel angry that they can do little about. In other words, the children come to recognize that their anger may be spurred on by problems they simply *can't* solve or change. In such cases, your task is to help the children realize they can learn to cope with the problem by accepting what they can't change, by learning to express their anger so that they can let it go, and by doing something good for themselves.

For example, a child who is angry over his or her parents' divorce—possibly due to a parent's chemical dependence—will be unable to do anything to change the divorce. To such a child, you might say: "Remember the three Cs? Just as a children can't cause, control, or cure a parent's chemical dependence, neither can they cause, control, or cure a parent's separation or divorce. Divorce is something children just have to accept. It's a grown-up decision that children can't change. But there are some helpful ways you can express your anger so you can let it go. You could write a letter to your parents—one you don't have to send—that tells them how angry you feel. Or you could use a special pillow and punch it until you don't feel so angry. You can also do something good for yourself. You could visit your grandma and play cards with her, or you could play with your favorite toys."

The idea that anger can be used as a positive force will be a new one for most of the children. Expect some misunderstanding and resistance. Be very active and accepting during the session's discussion. Acknowledge the children's ideas about ways to express anger, but gently correct and redirect any harmful ideas of expressing anger that they may express. Offer specific suggestions that are geared to the age and personalities of the children. For example: "Use your anger to give you power to control yourself when someone hits you" or "Use your anger to play football with more determination" or "Use your anger to get that social studies project started."

Children from chemically dependent families are amply supplied with anger. Teaching them how to use their anger is a great act of empowerment. This session begins the process of tapping into the power of anger. Session 7 focuses more on teaching the children a structured plan to help them choose helpful ways to express their anger so they can let it go.

Beginning the Session

Group Rules

Welcome the children warmly and pass out folders. Draw attention to the poster listing the group rules. Quickly review all the rules, calling on different children to read them one at a time.

1. I will keep what we talk about private. We call this confidentiality.
2. I will stay in my seat.
3. I will keep my hands to myself.
4. I will wait for my turn to talk, and I will listen carefully when others talk.
5. I won't tease or put other people down.
6. I can "pass" during go-arounds.
7. I will come to every group session.
8. I will make up any class work I miss.

Check for understanding before moving on.

Centering Exercise

Lead the children in a new centering exercise, "The Space Shuttle."

> This exercise will help you learn how to use your anger.

Close your eyes and relax. Imagine that you work for the people who send the space shuttle into outer space. You have an important job. You put the *fuel* into the space shuttle—the stuff that makes it go. The shuttle is parked and ready to go. It's going on a mission to help people in the world live peacefully together. All it needs is fuel—plenty of fuel—to get going.

This space shuttle uses a very special kind of fuel. It's not like the gas people put into a car. Instead, it needs a full tank of anger—*your* anger—to get off the ground.

Think of all the things that you've felt angry about today. *(Give specific examples appropriate to the group.)* Pump all that anger into the space shuttle tank.

Now think of all the things that you've felt angry about this past week. Pump all that anger into the shuttle.

Now think of all the things that you've felt angry about for the past year. Pump all that anger in.

By now you've been able to feel a lot of the anger you've felt in the past, and you've pumped all of it into the shuttle. It's loaded with fuel. It's ready to blast off into outer space.

The countdown is beginning: 5, 4, 3, 2, 1, blastoff! Look at it go! The mission is successful. You feel great because you've used your anger in a very important way. You feel free because you've been able to let go of your anger. You feel peaceful. You feel calmer and more relaxed than you've felt in a long, long time. You also feel proud because you used your anger to work for you.

Feelings Check-in

Do a feelings check-in with the children. Have them take their crayons and Feeling Wheels out of their folders. Direct the children to color in the section on the wheel that shows how they're feeling today. For younger children, read the names of the feelings on the wheel aloud (Angry [red], Scared [purple], Sad [blue], Glad [yellow]). The children can color in more than one feeling, since it's possible to have more than one feeling at a time. Tell the children that if they're having a feeling that is not named on the wheel, they can add a bubble to the outside of the wheel in any color they choose. Also point out that if they need to, the children can re-color a space.

When the children finish coloring, have a go-around, beginning with yourself. Invite each child to say his or her name and to show with the wheel how he or she is feeling. Be sure to accept each child's feeling(s) and to affirm each child. Ask the children to return the wheels to their folders.

Basic Facts Review

To help the children review the basic facts learned so far, show them Basic Facts Posters 1-10:

1. Chemical dependence is a <u>DISEASE</u>.
2. Alcohol and other drugs affect how people <u>ACT</u>, <u>THINK</u>, and <u>FEEL</u>, and how people <u>TREAT</u> you.
3. People with chemical dependence can't be cured, but they can get <u>BETTER</u>.
4. People can do things to feel <u>BETTER</u> without using alcohol or other drugs.
5. Children usually <u>LOVE</u> their parents, but since alcohol and other drugs affect how people act, think, feel, and treat you, children may not like how their parent <u>BEHAVES</u> when the parent uses alcohol or other drugs.
6. When someone is chemically dependent, it's nobody's <u>FAULT</u>.
7. The three **C**s are:
    1. Children don't <u>CAUSE</u> a parent to develop chemical dependence.
    2. Children can't <u>CONTROL</u> their parent's chemical dependence.
    3. Children can't <u>CURE</u> their parent's chemical dependence.
8. Children from chemically dependent families can:
    1. <u>LEARN</u> the facts about alcohol and other drugs.
    2. Ask for <u>HELP</u> for themselves.
    3. <u>RECOGNIZE</u>, <u>ACCEPT</u>, and <u>SHARE</u> their feelings.
9. Feelings aren't good or bad, or right or wrong; they just <u>ARE</u>.
10. Instead of swallowing feelings, it's better to <u>RECOGNIZE</u> them, <u>ACCEPT</u> them, and <u>SHARE</u> them with someone you trust.

In a go-around, ask a student to read the first fact aloud and to explain what it means. If a child has trouble, don't contradict or judge, simply clarify the explanation. Then ask all the children to repeat the fact together. Repeat the process for each fact.

Exploring the Story

The Story

Have the children settle themselves to hear the story. If you wish, let them hold onto their Peter the Puppy and Mrs. Owl puppets as they listen. Use the Peter the Puppy and Mrs. Owl toys to tell the story.

Hi, kids! How are you feeling today? No matter how you feel, I just want to say that your feelings are okay.

Do you remember the last time we met? I told you about the many different feelings I had. I told you how Mrs. Owl helped me *recognize, accept,* and *share* them with someone I trusted. Today I want to tell you about another time I met with Mrs. Owl. We talked about a feeling that I had every day. That feeling was anger. But when Mrs. Owl wanted to talk to me about anger, I didn't want to talk to her. I thought that she wouldn't like me if she knew how angry I felt. But I was wrong.

"Anger is a very normal feeling. All puppies get angry," Mrs. Owl told me. "Puppies are like people. They feel angry as often as twelve to fourteen times a day. Living in a family with chemical dependence might make a puppy feel angry even more often than that. So, Peter, why don't you tell me some things that make you feel angry?"

So I did. Here's what I told Mrs. Owl:

When I'm chasing cats in the park, and they get away from me, I feel ANGRY.

When I have a lot of homework or a big school project to do, I feel ANGRY.

When other puppies tease me and start fights, and *I* get sent to the principal's office, I feel ANGRY.

When my parents fight because of my dad's using alcohol and his chemical dependence, I feel ANGRY.

When my dad has been drinking beer and he yells at me, I feel ANGRY.

"Thank you," said Mrs. Owl. "Thank you for trusting me enough to tell me about your angry feelings. Would you like to learn some new ways to look at your anger?"

"Yes," I said. "I'd like it very much."

"Very good," said Mrs. Owl. "Now, whenever you feel angry, the first thing to do is to look at *why* you feel that way. Ask yourself, 'What's the problem that's making me feel angry?' Next, look carefully at the problem to see if it's one you can do something about or can *change*. If it's a problem you *can* change, then you can *use* your anger to work for you. You can use your anger to give you the energy or power to make changes in yourself."

"But what if it's a problem I can't change?" I asked.

"Oh, Peter," Mrs. Owl answered with a pleased smile, "I'm proud of you. You've used the three Cs to learn that there are some problems that you *can't* change or solve, then you have to remember the three Cs for help. Can you tell me what the three Cs are, Peter?" Mrs. Owl asked.

(Have the group join with Peter in reciting the three Cs:)

1. Children don't <u>C</u>AUSE a parent to develop chemical dependence.
2. Children can't <u>C</u>ONTROL their parent's chemical dependence.
3. Children can't <u>C</u>URE their parent's chemical dependence.

"Good!" said Mrs. Owl. "The three Cs can help you understand that there are some problems you just *can't* solve or change. But, you can do something instead. You can learn how to *cope* with them. Coping means handling a problem you can't change or solve.

"When you're angry because of a problem that you can't change, there are three things you can do to *cope* with the problem:

1. <u>ACCEPT</u> what you can't change.
2. <u>EXPRESS</u> your anger so you can let it <u>GO</u>.
3. Do something <u>GOOD</u> for yourself."

Mrs. Owl stopped and smiled. "Do you understand so far, Peter?" she asked. I must have had a funny look on my face, because she didn't wait for me to answer and shake my head no. Instead, Mrs. Owl just smiled again and said, "Okay, Peter, let's take a new look at the five things that you said made you feel angry. Let's see *why* they make you feel that way. Let's see what the problem is. Then let's see if it's a problem you can change. If you can, let's see how you can use your anger to work for you to give you the power to make changes in yourself. If it's a problem you can't change, then we'll look at ways to cope with it."

Mrs. Owl helped me see that feeling angry about the cats getting away from me is a problem I can solve. I just have to use my anger to give myself the power to run faster to catch the cats.

"Of course," Mrs. Owl laughed, "if you actually catch a cat, then you'll have another problem altogether."

Then, Mrs. Owl and I looked closely at why I get angry for getting sent to the principal's office for biting other puppies. We saw that this was also a problem I *can* change. Maybe I can't change those teasing puppies, but I can use my anger to change *myself*. Then I can tell those puppies who tease me, "Go chase yourselves. I'm not fighting with you." Or, I can just ignore them when they tease. I can use my anger to give me the power to control myself.

Mrs. Owl helped me see that having lots of homework or a project is not a problem I can change, but it is one I can make better. I can use my anger to give me the power to get going on the first step of the homework or project.

Then Mrs. Owl and I looked at why I felt angry when my parents fought about my dad's using alcohol and when my dad yells at me after he's been drinking. She said, "Peter, remember the three Cs. These are problems you *can't* change, but you can learn to *cope* with them."

Mrs. Owl helped me see that I can *accept* these problems by telling myself, "I'm not in charge of Mom and Dad, and I can't keep them from fighting" and "Dad's yelling at me not because he doesn't love me, but because he's been drinking. I can't change that. He probably still loves me even though he's yelling."

Then Mrs. Owl helped me see that I can *express* my anger so I could let it go. I used to express my anger by biting other puppies. But that was a harmful way of expressing anger, and that wasn't okay. Instead, Mrs. Owl helped me decide to express my anger so I could let it go by punching a pillow. Mrs. Owl also told me that I should *do something good for myself,* like reading a favorite book or playing with my best friends, Thomas Barker and the Labrador twins, Matt and Leigh.

Mrs. Owl showed me two good ways to handle my anger. I can use my anger to give me power to make changes in myself. Or, I can express my anger so I can let it go. I tried both these ways. They really help. Maybe you could try them, too.

The next time we meet, we'll be talking about more ways, helpful ways, to express anger so we can let it go.

Discussion

Lead a discussion to help group members better understand the facts—the key concepts—presented in the story. If you wish, let the children use their puppets when they speak, and let them hold the toy Peter the Puppy or Mrs. Owl. Go around the group, making sure that each child has an opportunity to add to the discussion. Encourage participation, but don't force it. Remember the group rule that allows a child to pass. Accept all ideas and answers, explaining or clarifying information where necessary to reinforce learning. To aid the discussion, you may use questions like the following:

- Is anger a normal feeling? (Yes. People—and puppies—feel angry as often as twelve to fourteen times a day.)

- What should you do when you feel angry? (Look at why you're feeling angry and decide if it's a problem you can change.)

- What should you do if it is a problem you can change? (Use anger to work for you—to give you the energy or power to make changes in yourself.)

- Can you think of any ways you can make your anger work for you? (Accept all reasonable answers; for example: use anger to help you run faster, to get you started on homework or a big project, or to control yourself instead of fighting.)

- What does *cope* mean? (Learning how to handle a problem you can't change or solve.)
- What should you do if you're feeling angry because of a problem you *can't* change? (Accept what you can't change. Express your anger so you can let it go. Do something good for yourself.)

Even if you choose not to use the above questions, make sure the discussion underscores these concepts.

Activity

Ask the children to retrieve their copies of Activity Sheet 7. Read aloud the title at the top of the sheet: "Anger at Work." Go through the directions with the youngsters, making sure they understand them. Give them time to draw a picture of a way to make their anger work for them or a way they can use their anger to make changes in themselves.

When the children finish, have a go-around. Invite each child to explain his or her drawing to the group. Take time to validate the children's angry feelings and to affirm them on finding helpful ways of making their anger work for them or using their anger to make changes in themselves. The children will learn more about dealing with—managing—anger in their next session. They will learn to choose helpful ways to express anger so they can let it go. Conclude by asking the children to place their drawings in their folders.

Basic Facts

Tell the children to take out Basic Facts Worksheet 6. Either read aloud the two new basic facts yourself, or have the children read them, one at a time.

11. When children are angry about a problem they can change, they should USE their anger to give them the power to make changes in themselves.

12. When children are angry about a problem they can't change, they should:

    1. ACCEPT what they can't change.

    2. EXPRESS their anger so they can let it GO.

    3. Do something GOOD for themselves.

Briefly discuss each fact, checking for understanding. Point out to the children how they encountered these facts in today's story.

Give the children time to complete the bottom half of the worksheet by filling in the blanks. Then have the group read the facts aloud. Have the children put their worksheets in their folders, along with their Peter the Puppy and Mrs. Owl puppets.

Wrapping Up

Centering Exercise

Settle the children and then repeat "The Space Shuttle."

Affirmation

Involve the group in an affirmation. Stand and join in a circle with the children, holding hands. Go around and have the children share ways they can make their anger work for them by making changes in themselves. Begin the affirmation yourself: "I can make anger work for me to make changes in myself by...."

Closing

Remain standing in a circle with the children, holding hands, and lead the group in the closing activity. Tell the children that you're going to make a *silent* wish for the child on your right. Then, when you've made the wish, *gently squeeze* the child's hand. The child makes a silent wish for the person on his or her right, then gently squeezes that child's hand, and so on. Continue around the circle until a wish and squeeze come back to you.

Collect the folders. Fill out a copy of the Process and Progress Form (see page 225) or the Progress Notes (see page 226) before leading the next session.

Session 7: Peter Learns to Manage Anger

Objectives

To help the children:

- understand that anger management is a way to cope with anger
- learn a seven-step plan for managing anger
- list ways of expressing anger
- discover helpful ways to express angry feelings

Session at a Glance

1. Group Rules: review—1 minute
2. Centering Exercise: "The Balloons"—3 minutes
3. Feelings Check-in: color Feeling Wheel—5 minutes
4. Basic Facts Review—6 minutes
5. The Story—9 minutes
6. Discussion—4 minutes
7. Activity: list helpful ways to express anger and illustrate one way (Activity Sheet 8)—8 minutes
8. Basic Facts: (Worksheet 7) read aloud; discuss; fill in blanks; read aloud together—2 minutes
9. Centering Exercise: repeat "The Balloons"—3 minutes
10. Affirmation: share a time when you were angry and an appropriate way to express that anger—3 minutes
11. Closing: have a silent wish and squeeze—1 minute

Preparation

- Display the posterboard copy of the group rules.

- Have the toy Peter the Puppy, the toy Mrs. Owl, and Basic Facts Posters 1-12 available.

- For Peter, print the steps of anger management on one side of a 4" x 8" index card. On the other side, print the following list of helpful ways to express anger: hammer nails into scrap wood, crumple old newspaper, punch a pillow, do jumping jacks, run laps around the house, write a paragraph about my anger, talk to someone I trust. Punch a hole in the top of the card. Use yarn to fasten it to Peter the Puppy's collar.

- Provide a 4" x 8" index card for each child; on each card write the list of seven anger management steps found on Basic Facts Worksheet 7.

- Make a poster. Across the top, print the title, "Steps to Managing Anger." Draw outlines of seven paw prints across the poster. (For a sample, see Activity Sheet 8.) With a marker write the steps of Anger Management in each paw print: RECOGNIZE, ACCEPT, RELAX, THINK, EVALUATE, CHOOSE, EXPRESS. (Note: Save the poster for use again in Session 8.)

- Make sure the children's folders contain the Feeling Wheel and pencils and crayons (including red, purple, blue, and yellow); then add the following materials to each folder:

    - a copy of Activity Sheet 8 ("Helpful Ways I Can Express Anger")

    - a copy of Basic Facts Worksheet 7

    - the 4" x 8" index card that you prepared listing the anger management steps

- Read through the session plan before meeting.

NOTES

Background and Guidelines

This session presents anger management steps that function as a cognitive behavioral technique; put simply, this session helps the children create a plan to express their anger in helpful ways. The plan shows the children how to put thinking *between* feeling angry and expressing anger.

As you lead the children through the session, help them become aware of the many different ways they can express their anger so they can let it go. Specific examples will be of great help: "One child I knew was angry about his parents' divorce, so he wrote them a letter, and he punched his pillow; in a little while, he didn't feel so angry" or "One time when I felt angry, I cleaned the bathroom, top to bottom. Then I went out and jogged." To help children evaluate the consequences of their expressions of anger, teach them to ask themselves: "Will this particular action be helpful or harmful?" During the session, you may notice that some children will describe harmful ways to express anger. Don't accept these harmful ways. Rather, gently encourage and redirect the children to find a helpful way of expressing their anger.

Emphasize to the children that the anger management plan is something they can use in real life: at home, on the playground, on the bus, and in the classroom. Let the children know that it's hard to change behavior right away. In fact, most people change their behavior quite slowly. Tell the children that they can help themselves change their behavior by going through the anger management steps, even *after* they choose a harmful way to express anger. Doing so can help them figure out what would have been a more helpful choice to express their anger so they could let it go. It often takes people six to ten weeks of processing the steps retroactively before they form the habit of using the plan *at the time of anger*.

Since children with behavioral problems may have difficulty in remembering the plan and its steps, and won't be able to change their behavior immediately, it's helpful to engage their teacher(s), principal, and student assistance team in using the plan. Work with teachers and children to set up a plan so that the children will know exactly what choices they have with regard to expressing their anger. Explosive children may benefit from a plan that includes helpful choices such as journal writing, playing with clay, sitting in a time-out chair in the office or with the guidance counselor, or drawing a picture. Help teachers to choose behaviors that will work in a particular classroom and encourage them to help the children implement their plans when they feel angry.

Beginning the Session

Group Rules

Welcome the children warmly and pass out folders. Draw attention to the poster listing the group rules. Quickly review all the rules, calling on different children to read them one at a time.

1. I will keep what we talk about private. We call this confidentiality.
2. I will stay in my seat.
3. I will keep my hands to myself.
4. I will wait for my turn to talk, and I will listen carefully when others talk.
5. I won't tease or put other people down.
6. I can "pass" during go-arounds.
7. I will come to every group session.
8. I will make up any class work I miss.

Check for understanding before moving on.

Centering Exercise

Lead the children in a new centering exercise, "The Balloons."

> In this centering exercise, you're going to experience some anger. Then you're going to express it in a helpful way. Finally, you'll be able to let it go.
>
> Imagine that you're very, very angry. Maybe you just had a terrible fight with your brother or sister. Maybe your parents were angry with you last night and hit you for no reason. Maybe your teacher said that you were talking in the classroom, but it was really the child who sits next to you.
>
> No matter the reason, right now, imagine how angry you feel. You feel very hot and like you have a lot of air in your chest. You're going to express that anger by blowing up some balloons.
>
> The first balloon that you pick up is a long, red one. Start blowing into that balloon. Blow all the anger you feel in your chest into that red balloon. *(Pause.)*
>
> Now pick up a round, blue balloon. You start to blow into it. You huff and puff. *(Pause.)*

Pick up a very big purple balloon. Blow and blow into it. *(Pause.)* By now you're feeling a bit better. You pick up a small, yellow balloon. You blow into it. Your air has magically turned into helium. You feel much lighter because you've put all of your anger into the balloons, and you've let your anger go. You feel calm and peaceful.

Feelings Check-in

Do a feelings check-in with the children. Have them take their crayons and Feeling Wheels out of their folders. Direct the children to color in the section on the wheel that shows how they're feeling today. For younger children, read the names of the feelings on the wheel aloud (Angry [red], Scared [purple], Sad [blue], Glad [yellow]). The children can color in more than one feeling, since it's possible to have more than one feeling at a time. Tell the children that if they're having a feeling that is not named on the wheel, they can add a bubble to the outside of the wheel in any color they choose. Also point out that if they need to, the children can re-color a space.

When the children finish coloring, have a go-around, beginning with yourself. Invite each child to say his or her name and to show with the wheel how he or she is feeling. Be sure to accept each child's feeling(s) and to affirm each child, paying special attention to anyone who mentions that he or she is feeling angry today. Ask the children to return the wheels to their folders.

Basic Facts Review

To help the children review the basic facts learned so far, show them Basic Facts Posters 1-12:

1. Chemical dependence is a <u>DISEASE</u>.

2. Alcohol and other drugs affect how people <u>ACT</u>, <u>THINK</u>, and <u>FEEL</u>, and how people <u>TREAT</u> you.

3. People with chemical dependence can't be cured, but they can get <u>BETTER</u>.

4. People can do things to feel <u>BETTER</u> without using alcohol or other drugs.

5. Children usually <u>LOVE</u> their parents, but since alcohol and other drugs affect how people act, think, feel, and treat you, children may not like how their parent <u>BEHAVES</u> when the parent uses alcohol or other drugs.

6. When someone is chemically dependent, it's nobody's <u>FAULT</u>.

7. The three **Cs** are:

    1. Children don't <u>CAUSE</u> a parent to develop chemical dependence.

    2. Children can't <u>CONTROL</u> their parent's chemical dependence.

    3. Children can't <u>CURE</u> their parent's chemical dependence.

8. Children from chemically dependent families can:
   1. <u>LEARN</u> the facts about alcohol and other drugs.
   2. Ask for <u>HELP</u> for themselves.
   3. <u>RECOGNIZE</u>, <u>ACCEPT</u>, and <u>SHARE</u> their feelings.
9. Feelings aren't good or bad, or right or wrong; they just <u>ARE</u>.
10. Instead of swallowing feelings, it's better to <u>RECOGNIZE</u> them, <u>ACCEPT</u> them, and <u>SHARE</u> them with someone you trust.
11. When children are angry about a problem they can change, they should <u>USE</u> their anger to give them the power to make changes in themselves.
12. When children are angry about a problem they can't change, they should:
    1. <u>ACCEPT</u> what they can't change.
    2. <u>EXPRESS</u> their anger so they can let it <u>GO</u>.
    3. Do something <u>GOOD</u> for themselves.

In a go-around, ask a student to read the first fact aloud and to explain what it means. If a child has trouble, don't contradict or judge, simply clarify the explanation. Then ask all the children to repeat the fact together. Repeat the process for each fact.

Exploring the Story

The Story

Have the children settle themselves to hear the story. If you wish, let them hold their Peter the Puppy and Mrs. Owl puppets. Use the Peter the Puppy and Mrs. Owl toys to tell the story.

> Hi, kids. I'm glad to see you. Can you remember the last time we talked? I said that I'd be telling you more about ways—helpful ways—to express anger so we can let it go. And that is just what I'm going to do.
>
> Do you remember how I told you how angry I felt when my dad used alcohol and then started yelling at me? Well, sometimes I was *really* angry at him. Sometimes, I felt that I hated him and wanted to bite him. Of course, I never did. Instead, I bit Milton or Crystal. But then my mom would yell at me and send me to my room. Sometimes, I felt so angry I would bite the other puppies at school. Then my teacher would send me to the principal's office.
>
> I was always getting into trouble. I didn't feel happy about what I was doing, but I didn't know how to change.

You see, I thought it was really wrong to feel angry toward my dad. I thought I was being bad for feeling like I hated him. So, I just got angry at the other puppies and bit them or swallowed down my feelings. That's why it was so hard for me to talk about this stuff to Mrs. Owl.

Well, you already know that I finally did tell Mrs. Owl about how I was feeling. She told me that my feelings weren't *wrong* and that I wasn't really a *bad* puppy. Mrs. Owl said that anger is a normal feeling to have, especially for a puppy growing up in a family where someone has the disease of chemical dependence.

"You probably don't really hate your dad," Mrs. Owl said. "It's the way he acts when he drinks that you hate."

Boy! I was glad to hear that!

Mrs. Owl reminded me that my anger came from a problem I couldn't solve, my dad's chemical dependence. "Because you can't solve that problem," she said, "you're trying to cope with your feelings of anger, but you're not having much luck. Instead of helping, the way you're coping—fighting and biting—is getting you into more and more trouble."

When Mrs. Owl said that, I must've looked pretty sad or ashamed, because she reached over, patted me on the head, and said, "I know about a better way of coping. It's a way called anger management. It's a plan to help you know what to do when you feel angry. Peter, would you like to learn how to manage your anger?"

"Yes!" I yelped.

"Good!" hooted Mrs. Owl. "Let's begin by taking a closer look at the way you've been coping. Now pay attention, Peter, to what you do. First, if your dad yells at you because he's been drinking, the first thing you do is feel angry. And that's okay. But what's the very next thing you do?"

"Well," I said, scratching behind an ear, "I usually bite someone."

"That's right," said Mrs. Owl. "You see, Peter, every time you start to feel angry, you rush right from *feeling* straight into *doing*. But, Peter, there's something missing in your way of coping. There's something that needs to go in between *feeling* angry thoughts and *doing* angry things. That something is *thinking*. You need a plan to help you put thinking between feeling and doing. You need a plan, Peter, for managing anger. 'Managing' means *knowing what steps to take* when you feel angry."

(Display the poster entitled "Steps to Managing Anger" and point out the seven paw prints. As Peter explains the following management plan, point to the name of each step.)

Mrs. Owl says that the first step in a plan for managing anger is to RECOGNIZE that I'm angry. It's like I have to say to myself, "I'm not feeling sad. I'm not feeling lonely. I'm feeling angry."

(Point to the word RECOGNIZE in the first paw print.)

The second step to take is to ACCEPT my anger. That means I have to see that anger is a normal feeling that puppies and people have, and that it's okay for me to have it.

(Point to the word ACCEPT in the second paw print.)

The third step is to PRACTICE a way of RELAXING. This means that I have to do something that makes me feel relaxed. You know, like breathing through my feet or the icicle.

(Point to the word RELAX in the third paw print.)

The fourth step of the plan is to THINK about the different ways I could express my anger. I could bite someone or punch a pillow or bark at someone.

(Point to the word THINK in the fourth paw print.)

The fifth step is to EVALUATE the consequences of the different ways I thought about expressing my anger. This means that when I think about a way to express my anger, I also have to think about what might happen next and whether it would be helpful or harmful. Like what might happen *after* I show my anger by biting (helpful or harmful?), or what might happen *after* I show my anger by barking at someone (helpful or harmful?).

(Point to the word EVALUATE in the fifth paw print.)

The sixth step is to CHOOSE a *helpful* way of expressing my anger.

(Point to the word CHOOSE in the sixth paw print.)

The final step is to EXPRESS my anger—to show it—in a helpful way.

(Point to the word EXPRESS in the seventh paw print.)

Look at all these steps. Let's read them together.

As Peter points to each step, encourage the children to read each aloud. Afterward, have Peter point to the fourth step, THINK, and continue the story.)

Mrs. Owl and I spent a lot of time together thinking about ways I could express my anger. She asked me to make a list of things I can do when I feel angry. I'll share my THINKING list with you, if you help me EVALUATE it. For each thing I tell you, show me a *thumbs up* if you think what might happen next would be *helpful*. But show me a *thumbs down* if what you think might happen next would be *harmful*.

These are some different ways I thought I could express my anger:

1. Chew on furniture. Helpful or harmful?
2. Bang the wall with a baseball bat. Helpful or harmful?
3. Hammer nails into scrap wood. Helpful or harmful?
4. Crumple old newspaper. Helpful or harmful?
5. Bite someone. Helpful or harmful?
6. Punch a pillow. Helpful or harmful?
7. Do jumping jacks. Helpful or harmful?
8. Bark at someone? Helpful or harmful?
9. Run away from home. Helpful or harmful?
10. Run laps around my house. Helpful or harmful?
11. Have a temper tantrum. Helpful or harmful?
12. Write a paragraph about my anger. Helpful or harmful?
13. Talk to someone I trust. Helpful or harmful?

Thanks for helping me evaluate my list for consequences of what might happen next. You helped me see that chewing on furniture, banging the wall with a bat, biting someone, running away from home, barking at someone, and having a temper tantrum could be *harmful*.

You also helped me see that hammering nails, crumpling old newspaper, punching a pillow, doing jumping jacks, running laps around the house, writing a paragraph about my anger, and talking to someone I trust could be *helpful*. I'll be sure to remember the help you gave me.

Before I go today, I'd like to tell you about last night. Something happened that gave me a chance to practice my steps for anger management.

My dad was helping me do my homework, when I made a mistake. My dad had been drinking, so he yelled at me and called me a stupid puppy. I started to feel all hot under the collar and sick as a dog. I felt very angry. I wanted to call my dad stupid and give him a nasty bite.

Instead, I remembered the plan and steps for managing my anger. I recognized that I was angry and accepted that it was okay to feel that way. I was so angry I had a hard time breathing, so I practiced a way of relaxing: I breathed through my feet—actually, through my paws! Then I remembered my list. I decided to go into my room and do twenty jumping jacks. After that, I told Harvey, my favorite toy boy, what my dad had done and how angry I felt. In a little while, I calmed down. I didn't feel so angry any more. Then I finished my homework by myself. I knew it wasn't a good time to ask my dad to help, since he'd been drinking, and the alcohol affected how he treated me.

The plan for managing my anger really worked well last night. But Mrs. Owl warned me that sometimes I might forget to use the steps of my plan. Then I might show my anger in a harmful way. But even if that happens, Mrs. Owl said that I should still go through the steps of the plan.

"It's hard for puppies to change their behavior right away, but practice makes perfect," Mrs. Owl said. "If you go through the steps often enough, it'll get easier and easier for you to remember to put thinking between feeling angry and expressing your anger. You'll be able to express your anger in helpful ways, so you can let it go."

That's why I'm wearing this card attached to my collar. I bet you were wondering what it was.

(Note: The card should list the steps of anger management on one side and Peter's helpful ways to express anger on the other side: hammer nails into scrap wood, crumple old newspaper, punch a pillow, do jumping jacks, run laps around the house, write a paragraph about anger, talk to someone you trust. See Preparation section.)

Well, on one side, it's the steps for anger management. There are a lot of steps, and this card helps me remember them. On the other side of the card is a list of the things I can do to express my anger in helpful ways: hammer nails into scrap wood, crumple old newspaper, punch a pillow, do jumping jacks, run laps around the house, write a paragraph about anger, talk to someone you trust. I keep the list with me to help me remember what to do when I feel angry, so I can express my anger and let it go. Mrs. Owl calls it my "license to chill." Get it? Maybe you can make a card like this.

Hmmm. But wait a minute, I see that none of you is wearing a collar. Well, I suppose you can still make a card. Then you could carry it in one of those funny things you *do* have called pockets.

Until we meet next time, remember, if you feel yourself getting hot under the collar, take the right steps to manage your anger so you can let it go.

Discussion

Lead a discussion to help group members better understand the facts—the key concepts—presented in the story. Let the children use their puppets when they speak, and let them hold Peter the Puppy or Mrs. Owl as they share. As the group discusses, remember to go around, making sure that each child has an opportunity to add to the discussion. Encourage participation, but don't force it. Remember the group rule that allows a child to pass. Accept all ideas and answers, explaining or clarifying information where necessary to reinforce learning. To aid the discussion, you may use questions like the following:

- Was it bad or wrong for Peter to feel angry when his dad yelled at him and called him names? (No. It's okay for Peter to feel angry. Besides, feelings aren't good or bad, or right or wrong. They just are.)
- Were fighting and biting helpful ways for Peter to express his anger? (No, they were harmful ways.)
- What does it mean to manage your anger? (It means having a plan to help you put thinking between feeling angry and doing angry things.)
- What are the steps of managing anger or anger management?

(Note: Allow the children to use the poster you made as they respond: recognize that you're angry; accept your anger; practice some form of relaxing; think about different ways to express your anger; evaluate consequences; choose the best way; express the anger in a helpful way.)

- What are some ways you might recognize that you're feeling angry? (Accept all responsible replies; look for examples like the following: you might get hot, blush, sweat, feel tense, feel your heart beating fast; breathe hard.)
- How do you accept anger? (Tell yourself it's okay to feel angry.)
- What are some ways you can relax? (Practice one of the centering exercises: "Breathing Through Your Feet," "The Icicle," "The Space Shuttle.")
- What are some ways to express anger? Are they helpful or harmful? (Accept all responsible replies; encourage the group to look to the examples Peter gave in the story.)
- What does it mean to *choose* a helpful way to express your anger? (To pick a way that doesn't harm yourself or anyone or anything else.)
- What does it mean to *express* your anger in a helpful way? (To go ahead and act—to do your best choice.)
- Why should you always try to express your anger in a helpful way? (So you can let go of your anger.)
- Should you expect to use these steps right away? (You should try. It's hard to change behavior right away. But if you keep using the steps, even after choosing a harmful way to express anger, doing so will help you to remember to put thinking between feelings and actions. Sooner or later, you'll use the steps when you're actually angry. But it may take two or three months and lots of practice. Don't give up.)

Even if you choose not to use the above questions, make sure the discussion underscores these concepts.

Activity

Ask the children to retrieve their copies of Activity Sheet 8. Read aloud the title at the top of the sheet: "Helpful Ways I Can Express Anger." Point out the seven paw prints on the sheet. Read aloud the key words for anger management, which are found inside the paw prints. Direct the children to list helpful ways they could express their anger under the paw prints. (Note: You may have to help younger children with writing.) Then ask them to choose one way they like and to illustrate it on Activity Sheet 8.

When the children finish, have a go-around. Invite each child to read from from his or her list and to explain his or her drawing to the group. Take time to affirm the children on finding helpful ways to express their anger. Have the children put their drawings in their folders.

Ask the children to retrieve the index card you prepared from their folders. Point out the anger management steps you've written for them on one side of the card. Then give them a moment or two to copy their lists of helpful ways they could express their anger on the other side of the card. Offer help to younger children. Tell the youngsters that they can keep their card and carry it in their pocket. Whenever they feel angry, they should look at the card to help them put thinking between feeling and action.

Basic Facts

Tell the children to take out Basic Facts Worksheet 7. Either read aloud the two new basic facts yourself, or have the children read them, one at a time.

13. Anger management is a way to COPE with anger.

14. The anger management steps are:

    1. RECOGNIZE that you're angry.

    2. ACCEPT your anger.

    3. PRACTICE some RELAXATION.

    4. THINK about ways to express the anger.

    5. EVALUATE the consequences.

    6. CHOOSE the best way.

    7. EXPRESS the anger in a helpful way.

By this time, the children should be very familiar with these facts. Even so, spend some time going through them, briefly discussing each fact and checking for understanding. Then have the children fill in the blanks on the bottom half of the worksheet. Finally, ask the group to read the facts aloud. Have the children put their worksheets in their folders, along with their Peter the Puppy and Mrs. Owl puppets.

Wrapping Up

Centering Exercise

Settle the children and then repeat "The Balloons."

Affirmation

Involve the group in an affirmation. Stand and join in a circle with the children, holding hands. Go around and have the children share a time they felt angry and a helpful way they expressed—or could have expressed—their anger. Begin the affirmation yourself: "One time that I got angry was.... A helpful way to express my angry feeling would have been...."

Closing

Remain standing in a circle with the children, holding hands, and lead the group in the closing activity. Tell the children that you're going to make a *silent* wish for the child on your right. Then, when you've made the wish, *gently squeeze* the child's hand. The child makes a silent wish for the person on his or her right, then gently squeezes that child's hand, and so on. Continue around the circle until a wish and squeeze come back to you.

Collect the folders. Fill out a copy of the Process and Progress Form (see page 225) or the Progress Notes (see page 226) before leading the next session.

Session 8: Peter Learns Other Coping Strategies

Objectives

To help the children:

- recognize that they can draw on the facts they have learned to help them cope in stressful situations
- identify coping strategies
- understand that they can't fix their parents' problems, but they can take care of themselves
- learn to wait until a person is sober before sharing feelings

Session at a Glance

1. Group Rules: review—1 minute
2. Centering Exercise:"The Waterfall"—3 minutes
3. Feelings Check-in: color Feeling Wheel—5 minutes
4. Basic Facts Review—7 minutes
5-7. The Story—Discussion—Activity: discover, discuss and write coping strategies (Activity Sheet 9)—20 minutes
8. Basic Facts: (Worksheet 8) read aloud; discuss; fill in blanks; read aloud together—2 minutes
9. Centering Exercise: repeat "The Waterfall"—3 minutes
10. Affirmation: share coping strategies—3 minutes
11. Closing: have a silent wish and squeeze—1 minute

Preparation

- Display the posterboard copy of the group rules.

- Have the toy Peter the Puppy, the toy Mrs. Owl, and Basic Facts Posters 1-14 available.

- Make sure the children's folders contain the Feeling Wheel and pencils and crayons (including red, purple, blue, and yellow); then add the following materials to each folder:

    - a copy of Activity Sheet 9 ("Coping Strategies")

    - a copy of Basic Facts Worksheet 8

- Have available the poster "Steps to Managing Anger" that you made for Session 7. (Note: If you plan to use the optional Session 10, retain this poster.)

- Read through the session plan before meeting.

NOTES

Background and Guidelines

One of the most difficult issues for children from chemically dependent families is learning to accept their inability to solve their family's problems, namely: to stop a parent's use of alcohol or other drugs. Group leaders like you also face this problem. You cannot solve the children's family problems, or the problems of the children themselves. Accepting this is the beginning of detachment (see Background and Guidelines for Session 4).

In this session, the children begin to own the concepts and facts they've learned in previous sessions and begin to apply them to their lives. They will use the disease concept, the three Cs and the three steps in this session. You will need to draw on your understanding of co-dependence, detachment, and empowerment to help the children. You will also be helping them apply the basic facts in real-life scenarios.

The session helps the children begin to detach themselves from their family's problems. Because children love their parents, this is no simple task. They will need your understanding, encouragement, and reassurance that they aren't acting selfishly. They can care about others, their parents included, but they can't fix a grown-up's problems. Many at-risk children, however, really believe they can fix their parents' problems. And parents of at-risk children frequently, and misguidedly, seek help, emotional and otherwise, from their children. Such children need your help to see that only an adult can fix adult problems, that although it's okay for their parents to need help, they should get it from another adult.

Therefore, the children should understand that when Mrs. Owl teaches Peter to take care of himself, she is not counseling selfishness. Rather, she is urging self-preservation. Like Peter, the children need to take responsibility for handling their feelings in helpful ways. Doing so frees them to solve problems and to cope with those problems they can't solve. Remember, living in a chemically dependent family is difficult, frustrating, and unfair. The children will feel deeply about this situation and want to change it. They can't. They can, however, refuse to accept the responsibility for the disease of chemical dependence or for its effects on the family. This frees the children of a terrible burden and lets them use their energy to achieve personal goals.

It's important to help the children recognize that although they have no power over their family's problems, they do have power to make things better for themselves. They can decide what they want to achieve and feel good enough about themselves to take steps to attain their goals.

Note that the flow of this session differs slightly from that of earlier ones. As in previous sessions, this session's second stage, *Exploring the Story*, includes the story, discussion, activity, and basic facts. However, the first three elements of this stage (story, discussion, and activity) don't function as separate elements. Rather, they are combined in a way that allows the children to draw on the story's material directly as they discuss and apply the basic facts and concepts in the story to create effective coping strategies. Therefore, as you read over the following plan, you may wish to give some extra attention to the *Exploring the Story* stage.

Beginning the Session

Group Rules

Welcome the children warmly and pass out folders. Draw attention to the poster listing the group rules. Quickly review all the rules, calling on different children to read them one at a time.

1. I will keep what we talk about private. We call this confidentiality.
2. I will stay in my seat.
3. I will keep my hands to myself.
4. I will wait for my turn to talk, and I will listen carefully when others talk.
5. I won't tease or put other people down.
6. I can "pass" during go-arounds.
7. I will come to every group session.
8. I will make up any class work I miss.

Check for understanding before moving on.

Centering Exercise

Lead the children in a new centering exercise, "The Waterfall."

> Close your eyes and relax. Pretend that you're walking on a beautiful path in the mountains. You're taking a hike down the mountain. It's October, and the sky is clear and a deep shade of blue. The air is cool, but the sun is warm. The leaves are changing colors. Look at the beautiful shades of red, orange, and yellow. Imagine what the orange and yellow leaves look like as you look up and see them like lace against the sky.
>
> You keep walking down the mountain path until you come upon a waterfall, a beautiful cascading waterfall, a stream tumbling down over huge boulders. You sit on a boulder near the waterfall, and you empty your mind. You pay attention to the sound of the water as it rushes over the boulders and trickles down the stream. You imagine that the water is rushing over you and making you feel clean and refreshed.

As you sit quietly on the boulder, you drink in the warmth of the sun. You see leaves that have fallen into the stream. They float like tiny boats on the bubbling water. You decide to put all your worries, problems, and frustrations on the leaves and to let them all float away.

So if you're worried because *(use appropriate examples specific to the children in your group, such as . . .)* you don't have your homework finished that's due today, let that worry float away on a leaf. Or, if you had a fight on the bus this morning, and you're afraid you might get suspended, put that worry on a leaf and let it float away. Or, if you feel angry over your mom's yelling at you because she didn't like the outfit you put on this morning, put that anger on a leaf and watch it float away.

Put all your worries, problems, and frustrations on leaves and watch them all float away. Soon they're all gone. When you open your eyes, you're going to be able to work hard because all your problems have floated away. You can go back and solve these problems later.

Feelings Check-in

Do a feelings check-in with the children. Have them take their crayons and Feeling Wheels out of their folders. Direct the children to color in the section on the wheel that shows how they're feeling today. For younger children, read the names of the feelings on the wheel aloud (Angry [red], Scared [purple], Sad [blue], Glad [yellow]). The children can color in more than one feeling, since it's possible to have more than one feeling at a time. Tell the children that if they're having a feeling that is not named on the wheel, they can add a bubble to the outside of the wheel in any color they choose. Also point out that if they need to, the children can re-color a space.

When the children finish coloring, have a go-around, beginning with yourself. Invite each child to say his or her name and to show with the wheel how he or she is feeling. Be sure to accept each child's feeling(s) and to affirm each child. Ask the children to return the wheels to their folders.

Basic Facts Review

To help the children review the basic facts learned so far, show them Basic Facts Posters 1-14:

1. Chemical dependence is a DISEASE.
2. Alcohol and other drugs affect how people ACT, THINK, and FEEL, and how people TREAT you.
3. People with chemical dependence can't be cured, but they can get BETTER.
4. People can do things to feel BETTER without using alcohol or other drugs.

5. Children usually <u>LOVE</u> their parents, but since alcohol and other drugs affect how people act, think, feel, and treat you, children may not like how their parent <u>BEHAVES</u> when the parent uses alcohol or other drugs.

6. When someone is chemically dependent, it's nobody's <u>FAULT</u>.

7. The three Cs are:

    1. Children don't <u>C</u>AUSE a parent to develop chemical dependence.

    2. Children can't <u>C</u>ONTROL their parent's chemical dependence.

    3. Children can't <u>C</u>URE their parent's chemical dependence.

8. Children from chemically dependent families can:

    1. <u>LEARN</u> the facts about alcohol and other drugs.

    2. Ask for <u>HELP</u> for themselves.

    3. <u>RECOGNIZE</u>, <u>ACCEPT</u>, and <u>SHARE</u> their feelings.

9. Feelings aren't good or bad, or right or wrong; they just <u>ARE</u>.

10. Instead of swallowing feelings, it's better to <u>RECOGNIZE</u> them, <u>ACCEPT</u> them, and <u>SHARE</u> them with someone you trust.

11. When children are angry about a problem they can change, they should <u>USE</u> their anger to give them the power to make changes in themselves.

12. When children are angry about a problem they can't change, they should:

    1. <u>ACCEPT</u> what they can't change.

    2. <u>EXPRESS</u> their anger so they can let it <u>GO</u>.

    3. Do something <u>GOOD</u> for themselves.

13. Anger management is a way to <u>COPE</u> with anger.

14. The anger management steps are:

    1. <u>RECOGNIZE</u> that you're angry.

    2. <u>ACCEPT</u> your anger.

    3. <u>PRACTICE</u> some <u>RELAXATION</u>.

    4. <u>THINK</u> about ways to express the anger.

    5. <u>EVALUATE</u> the consequences.

    6. <u>CHOOSE</u> the best way.

    7. <u>EXPRESS</u> the anger in a helpful way.

In a go-around, ask a student to read the first fact aloud and to explain what it means. If a child has trouble, don't contradict or judge, simply clarify the explanation. Then ask all the children to repeat the fact together. Repeat the process for each fact.

Exploring the Story

The Story—Discussion—Activity

Settle the children to hear the story. If you wish, invite them to hold onto their Peter the Puppy and Mrs. Owl puppets. Use the Peter the Puppy and Mrs. Owl toys to tell the story.

Hi, girls and boys! I'm glad to see you here. The last time we met, we talked about anger management and learned that it is a way of *coping* with feelings of anger. Remember, *coping* means learning how to handle a problem you can't change or solve. Then we learned a seven-step plan for managing angry feelings. Let's look at the plan again.

(Display the "Steps to Managing Anger" poster made for Session 7.)

Mrs. Owl showed me that I can use the basic facts to help me handle other problems—besides feelings of anger—I can't change or solve.

"You live with someone who has the disease of chemical dependence, don't you, Peter?" Mrs. Owl asked me.

"Yes, I do," I said. "My dad has chemical dependence."

"Well, you know," Mrs. Owl went on, "sometimes things might happen in your family that make you feel very uncomfortable. Very often, there will be nothing you can do about those things—they'll be problems you can't change or solve. *But* you can learn strategies to cope with those things. Do you know what a *strategy* is, Peter?"

"Unh, uh," I said, shaking my head.

"A strategy is a way or plan for doing something," Mrs. Owl explained. "So, a coping strategy is a way or plan to handle a problem you can't change or solve."

"Oh, I get it," I said. "Well, at least I think I get it."

"I'll tell you what, Peter," said Mrs. Owl. "I'll help you figure out some coping strategies. To begin, why don't you tell me about something that might happen in your home that would make you feel very uncomfortable?"

It only took me a second to think of something that happens in my house that makes me feel uncomfortable a lot. So I told Mrs. Owl, "Sometimes, my dad and mom have terrible fights. Sometimes, they even throw things at each other. Whenever that happens, I try to get them to stop, but then they get angry at me."

"Okay, Peter, why do you think your parents fight?" Mrs. Owl asked.

"I think it's because my dad is sick with chemical dependence," I said.

"I think you're absolutely right, Peter," Mrs. Owl said. "Now, remember Basic Fact 2. Your parents are probably fighting because the disease of chemical dependence affects how people act, think, and feel, and how they treat others. So, when your parents are fighting, do you think there's any way *you* can get them to stop? Now, wait, Peter. Before you answer, think of the three Cs."

I did what Mrs. Owl asked. I stopped and thought of the three Cs. Let's say the three Cs together.

(Have Peter lead the group in reciting the three Cs:)

1. Children don't CAUSE a parent to develop chemical dependence.

2. Children can't CONTROL their parent's chemical dependence.

3. Children can't CURE their parent's chemical dependence.

After thinking for a minute, I answered Mrs. Owl. "No," I said, "I guess I can't stop my parents from fighting."

Then Mrs. Owl asked, "Could you change or solve the problems your parents are having—the problems that make them fight?"

I remembered the three Cs again and answered, "No, children can't solve their parents' problems."

"That's right!" Mrs. Owl hooted. "You can't solve your parents' problems. Who can solve your parents' problems, Peter?"

"I guess only my parents can solve their problems," I answered.

"That's also right," Mrs. Owl said. "Parents may need to ask for help, too. But they should ask another grown-up for help. Even though you can't take care of your parents, you can take care of yourself, can't you, Peter?"

"Yes, I can," I said with a smile.

"Indeed, you can," said Mrs. Owl. "So let's you and I decide on some ways you can handle this problem you can't change or solve. Let's decide on some things you can do to take care of yourself."

And so we did. We decided on a *coping strategy* I could use when my parents fight. Here it is:

1. I realize and accept that I can't make my parents stop fighting. It's not a puppy's job, and I wouldn't succeed anyway.

2. I'll go to a safe place where I won't get hurt. I like to go to my bedroom and play with Harvey, my toy boy.

Can you think of any other coping strategy I could use when my parents fight?

(Break here for **Discussion** and **Activity**.)

Lead a discussion on the first part of the story to help the children think of another coping strategy for Peter. To aid the discussion, you may use questions like the following:

- What was the first problem situation Peter talked to Mrs. Owl about? (His parents fight and throw things at each other.)

- What basic fact helped Peter see *why* his parents fought? (Basic Fact 2 reminded Peter that the disease of chemical dependence affects how people act, think, feel, and treat others. Peter's parents fought because of his dad's chemical dependence.)

- What basic fact helped Peter see that he *couldn't* get his parents to stop fighting? (The three Cs, Basic Fact 7: children don't CAUSE a parent to develop chemical dependence; children can't CONTROL their parent's chemical dependence; children can't CURE their parent's chemical dependence.)

- Even though Peter couldn't solve his parents' problem (make them stop fighting), could he do anything for *himself*? (Yes, he could make a coping strategy.)

- What is a coping strategy? (A way or plan to handle a problem you can't change or solve.)

- What were the two parts of Peter's coping strategy to use when his parents fought? (1. Realize and accept that he can't make his parents stop fighting. It's not a puppy's job, and he wouldn't succeed anyway. 2. Go to a safe place where he won't get hurt—to his bedroom—and play with Harvey, his toy boy.)

- What are some other coping ideas Peter might use?

To help the children answer this final question, ask them to take their copies of Activity Sheet 9 out of their folders. Draw attention to "Problem Situation 1" on the sheet and read it aloud. Direct the children to write their ideas for another coping strategy for Peter in the space provided on the sheet. (Note: You may have to help younger children with writing.)

When the children finish writing, have a go-around, allowing them to tell what they wrote. Make sure that their suggestions reflect an understanding that children can't solve parents' problems, but that they can take care of themselves. Afterward, return to the story, where Peter will set up another problem situation that calls for another coping strategy.

(Continue with *Peter* telling the **Story**.)

Thanks for your strategies, guys. Maybe I'll try your ideas for coping if my parents ever have another terrible fight. But don't go away yet. I had another problem situation that needed a coping strategy. So I told Mrs. Owl about it.

"Sometimes," I told her, "when it's late at night, and my dad is not home yet, I hear my mom crying."

"Why do you think she cries?" Mrs. Owl asked. "Do you think she could be worried that your dad is out drinking, and maybe she's feeling afraid or angry?"

"I guess that's probably it," I said. "But it makes me feel sad."

"I'm sure it does, Peter," said Mrs. Owl, "but can you solve your mom's problem? Can you stop her from worrying or take away her anger?"

"No," I said.

"Right!" said Mrs. Owl. "Who is the only person who can do what needs to be done for your mom to feel better, Peter?

"I guess she's the only one who can work to solve her problems, but I want to make her feel better."

"I know you do, Peter," Mrs. Owl said with a sad smile, "but remember what you know about feelings. The worry or anger aren't your feelings. They belong to your mom. Only *she* can do what needs to be done to feel better. She may need to ask for help, and that's okay. But your mom needs to ask another grown-up for help"

"Okay," I said, "but can't I tell my mom how I'm feeling? Can't I tell her that I'm feeling sad for her and that I love her?"

"You most certainly can, Peter," Mrs. Owl told me. "You can remember the basic facts that tell you to recognize, accept, and share your feelings. You can share them with your mom."

"And I can share them with someone else I trust, can't I, Mrs. Owl?" I asked. "I could share them with Harvey, my toy boy."

"Yes, Peter," said Mrs. Owl, "and you can also do something good for yourself. Never forget, Peter, you have power to make things better for yourself, even if you can't fix your mom's problem. So let's you and I decide on a coping strategy to help you if you ever hear your mom crying late at night again."

Mrs. Owl helped me with a new coping strategy. Here it is:

1. I give my mom a big hug and tell her I'm sorry that she's feeling sad. Then I tell her that I love her.

2. I do something that makes me feel good, like drawing a picture.

3. I tell someone I trust that I feel sad and scared when my mom cries.

4. I practice a way to relax. I paint a picture in my mind of a warm, safe place.

Mrs. Owl said that it's *not* being selfish to take care of myself. I still love my parents a whole bunch, just like you love yours. But puppies like me and children like you have to keep working at handling our own feelings. We have to solve our own problems. And we have to find strategies to cope with the problems we can't solve.

(Break here for **Discussion** and **Activity**.)

Lead a discussion on the second part of the story to help the children think of another coping strategy for Peter. To aid the discussion, you may use questions like the following:

- What was the second problem situation Peter needed a coping strategy for? (Sometimes late at night when his dad isn't home yet, he hears his mom crying.)

- Why do you think Peter's mom cries? (She could be worried that Peter's dad is out drinking alcohol; also, maybe she's feeling afraid or angry.)

- Why is it impossible for Peter to make his mom feel better? (Because his mom's feelings belong to her; only she can do what needs to be done in order to feel better.)

- Is there anyone Peter can make feel better? (Yes, himself. He can recognize and accept his feelings of sadness and share them with someone he trusts. He can also do something good for himself.)

- What were the four parts of Peter's coping strategy to use when his mom cried late at night?

   (1. Give his mom a big hug and tell her that he's sorry she's feeling sad. Then tell her that he loves her.

   2. Do something that makes him feel better, like drawing a picture.

   3. Tell someone he trusts that he feels sad and scared when his mom cries.

   4. Practice a way to relax. Paint a picture in his mind of a warm, safe place.)

- Do you think Peter is being selfish if he won't try to make his mom feel better? (Look for answers that show the children understand that it's not being selfish to take care of themselves. While children love their parents, they can't change them. They have to work at handling their own feelings, solving their own problems, and finding strategies to cope with the problems they can't solve.)

Have the children look at "Problem Situation 2" on their copies of Activity Sheet 9. Direct the children to write their ideas for another coping strategy for Peter in the space provided on the sheet. (Note: You may have to help younger children with writing.)

When the children finish writing, have a go-around, allowing them to tell what they wrote. Again, make sure that their suggestions reflect an understanding that only parents can solve parents' problems, and that when children take care of themselves, they're not acting selfishly, but are showing self-preservation. Afterward, return to the story, where Peter will set up a final problem situation that calls for another coping strategy.

(Continue with *Peter* telling the **Story**.)

You guys have some really good ideas about coping with problem situations. Maybe you could listen to one more. It's a problem situation that comes up for me a lot.

"I really love to play games," I told Mrs. Owl, "and one of my favorite games is playing fetch with my dad. We really have a good time. But sometimes when my dad has promised to play fetch with me, instead he's asleep on the couch from drinking too much alcohol."

"Oh, Peter," said Mrs. Owl, "that must be hard for you. What do you do when that happens?"

"Well, sometimes I try barking to wake him up," I said. "But he gets pretty angry when I do that. He won't play fetch. Instead, he yells at me."

"Peter, why do you think your dad sleeps after drinking alcohol? And why do you think he yells at you?" Mrs. Owl asked calmly.

I thought for a while and finally remembered Basic Fact 2. "Well," I said, "alcohol and other drugs affect how people act, think, feel, and treat you. Maybe alcohol makes my dad act the way he does."

"Good for you, Peter," said Mrs. Owl. "Your dad might be very sleepy after drinking alcohol. And when people—and dogs like your dad—drink alcohol, they're often angrier than when they don't drink.

"There's something important for you to learn, Peter. Since alcohol and other drugs affect how people act, think, feel, and treat you, it's best for others to wait until the people who use alcohol or other drugs are sober before discussing feelings or anything else important."

I asked Mrs. Owl what sober means.

"Someone is sober when they have not taken alcohol or other drugs," Mrs. Owl replied. "When someone does use alcohol or other drugs, it may take an evening, a night, or even a whole other day for the effects of the alcohol or other drug to wear off. Until that happens, the person is not sober.

"If your dad is using alcohol, it's affecting his *thinking*," Mrs. Owl went on. "So, when he's drinking it's probably not a good time to ask for his help with homework. When your dad is drinking, it's also affecting his *feelings*, so it's not a good time to share your feelings with your dad. It will be much better to wait until he's sober, when the effects of the alcohol wear off, before asking for help with homework or discussing feelings.

"But let's get back to your problem about playing fetch," Mrs. Owl said. "When your dad breaks a promise to play fetch with you, how do you feel?" she asked.

I thought for a moment, then answered, "I feel angry. But, at the same time, I also feel sad and lonely, because I really wanted to play fetch."

"Well, Peter, what can you do with your anger?" Mrs. Owl asked.

I remembered my steps for managing anger. "I can wait until my dad is sober," I said. "Then I can tell him that I was disappointed that we couldn't play fetch because he was asleep."

"That's great!" said Mrs. Owl. "Now what can you do with your feelings of sadness and loneliness? Do you have to stay sad and lonely all day?"

I thought some more. I remembered that there are lots of things that I can do to make me feel better. "I can ask Milton to play fetch with me," I said. "Or, I can ask my friends, Thomas Barker and the Labrador twins, Matthew and Leigh, to chase cats with me in the park."

"I'm proud of you, Peter," Mrs. Owl told me. "You're really using the basic facts you've learned. You *can* do things to feel better."

Here's the third coping strategy Mrs. Owl and I made up:

1. I ask Milton to play fetch with me.
2. I do something else I enjoy, like chasing cats with Thomas Barker and the Labrador twins, Matthew and Leigh.
3. The next day, before my dad has had any alcohol to drink, I tell him that I felt disappointed that we couldn't play fetch because he was asleep.

Knowing the basic facts helped me make my coping strategies for problem situations. Whenever you're in a problem situation, just remember the basic facts. Then you can come up with a coping strategy to help you, too.

(Break here for **Discussion** and **Activity**.)

Lead a discussion on the third part of the story to help the children think of a final coping strategy for Peter. To aid the discussion, you may use questions like the following:

- What happens to a person who's been using alcohol or other drugs? (If the children have difficulty answering, refer them to Basic Fact 2: "Alcohol and other drugs affect how people ACT, THINK, and FEEL, and how people TREAT you." Help the children see that Barnaby's thinking and feelings may be affected when he's using alcohol. If Peter tries to talk to his dad, he may forget things or get angry.)

- Do you think Peter should try to talk to his dad when he's been using alcohol? (No, it's better if Peter waits until his dad is sober, when the effects of alcohol have worn off, before talking to him.)
- If Peter is feeling angry or upset with his dad, what can Peter do? (Look for responses that show the children understand that Peter can recognize, accept, and share his feelings; that Peter can do something good for himself; or he can follow his steps for anger management.)

Have the children look at "Problem Situation 3" on their copies of Activity Sheet 9. Direct the children to write their ideas for a final coping strategy for Peter in the space provided on the sheet. (Note: You may have to help younger children with writing.)

When the children finish writing, have a go-around, allowing them to tell what they wrote. Again, make sure that their suggestions reflect an understanding of the anger management steps, Basic Fact 4 (People can do things to feel BETTER without using alcohol or other drugs), and the new basic fact, Basic Fact 17, presented in the story (Children should WAIT until a chemically dependent parent is sober before talking about how they feel).

Affirm the children on the ways they've been putting the facts they've learned into action. Be sure to tell the youngsters to put their sheets safely in their folders.

Basic Facts

Ask the children to take out Basic Facts Worksheet 8. Either read aloud the three new basic facts yourself, or have the children read them, one at a time.

15. Children can't FIX their parent's problems.
16. Children can take GOOD CARE of themselves.
17. Children should WAIT until a chemically dependent parent is sober before talking about how they feel.

Point out that the children have already encountered these facts in today's session. Briefly discuss each fact, checking for understanding.

Give the children time to complete the bottom half of the worksheet by filling in the blanks. Then have the group read the facts aloud. Have the children place their worksheets in their folders, along with their Peter the Puppy and Mrs. Owl puppets.

Wrapping Up

Centering Exercise

Settle the children and then repeat "The Waterfall."

Affirmation

Involve the group in an affirmation. Stand and join in a circle with the children, holding hands. Go around and have the children share ideas for coping strategies. Begin the affirmation yourself: "One coping strategy I can use is. . . ."

Closing

Remain standing in a circle with the children, holding hands, and lead the group in the closing activity. Tell the children that you're going to make a *silent* wish for the child on your right. Then, when you've made the wish, *gently squeeze* the child's hand. The child makes a silent wish for the person on his or her right, then gently squeezes that child's hand, and so on. Continue around the circle until a wish and squeeze come back to you.

Collect the folders. Fill out a copy of the Process and Progress Form (see page 225) or the Progress Notes (see page 226) before leading the next session.

Note: If you have decided to use the optional Session 10, look ahead to it *now* to make plans for the children's presentation. Check out school schedules and available audiences. Be ready to talk briefly about the presentation at the conclusion of Session 9 to inform the children about the times for practicing and giving the presentation.

Session 9: Peter Learns How to Take Care of Himself

Objectives

To help the children:

- discover that they need to make good choices
- set goals to take care of their bodies, feelings, minds, and choices

Session at a Glance

1. Group Rules: review—1 minute
2. Centering Exercise: "The Rainbow"—3 minutes
3. Feelings Check-in: color Feeling Wheel—5 minutes
4. Basic Facts Review—8 minutes
5. The Story—4 minutes
6. Discussion—4 minutes
7. Activity: write personal goals for caring for self (Activity Sheet 10)—11 minutes
8. Basic Facts: (Worksheet 9) read aloud; discuss; fill in blanks; read aloud together—2 minutes
9. Centering Exercise: repeat "The Rainbow"—3 minutes
10. Affirmation: share a way you can take care of yourself—3 minutes
11. Closing: have a silent wish and squeeze—1 minute

Preparation

- Display the posterboard copy of the group rules.
- Have the toy Peter the Puppy, the toy Mrs. Owl, and Basic Facts Posters 1-17 available.
- Make sure the children's folders contain the Feeling Wheel and pencils and crayons (including red, purple, blue, and yellow); then add the following materials to each folder:
    - a copy of Activity Sheet 10 ("My Personal Goals")
    - a copy of Basic Facts Worksheet 9
- Optional: Make a poster listing Peter's personal goals (see the story and Activity Sheet 10).
- Have sheets of stiff, colored construction paper and paste or glue sticks for each child.
- Read through the session plan before meeting.

_____

NOTES

Background and Guidelines

In this session, Peter models for the children how to give up responsibility for their family's disease and problems. Peter helps them learn how to assume age-appropriate responsibility for themselves by setting personal goals. The children are encouraged to take good care of themselves and make good decisions for themselves in the areas of body, mind, feelings, and choices.

As leader, you will not be recommending that the children abandon their families, leave home, and get a job. Rather, you need to encourage them to set their sights on age-appropriate responsibilities. For example, even kindergarten children can decide to eat healthful foods and go to school every day; older children can decide to try to get on the honor roll.

When you discuss goals regarding feelings, remember that children can't control the feelings they get. However, children can be responsible for what they do with their feelings. For instance, children could wallow in feelings and be overwhelmed by them, or they could decide to choose an appropriate coping strategy to deal with them, such as talking about their feelings with someone they trust or doing something that will help them feel better. Emphasize again to the children that although they can't fix their family's problems, they can do things that will help them better cope with those problems.

For each of the areas of body, mind, feelings, and choices, help the children set goals that are positive and attainable. For example, in the area of feelings, a goal such as "I will feel happy all the time" is neither positive nor attainable. A better goal would be "I will talk to a trusted friend whenever I feel upset."

The children are asked to share goals verbally because sharing helps them assume ownership. With positive feedback from you and other group members, sharing also empowers the children to take the steps necessary to achieve their goals.

The story introduces the no-use rule regarding alcohol and other drugs. Statistically, children who have a parent with chemical dependence are more susceptible to developing this disease than are children from homes where the disease isn't present. Children can make sure that they will not develop the disease by choosing not to use alcohol or other drugs at all. People don't approach their first use of alcohol or other drugs with the thought of developing chemical dependence. However, if people *never* use alcohol or other drugs, they will never become chemically dependent. Thus, it is highly recommended that the children decide to make it a personal goal not to use alcohol or other drugs.

Beginning the Session

Group Rules

Welcome the children warmly, pass out folders, and draw attention to the poster listing the group rules. Quickly review all the rules, calling on different children to read them one at a time.

1. I will keep what we talk about private. We call this confidentiality.
2. I will stay in my seat.
3. I will keep my hands to myself.
4. I will wait for my turn to talk, and I will listen carefully when others talk.
5. I won't tease or put other people down.
6. I can "pass" during go-arounds.
7. I will come to every group session.
8. I will make up any class work I miss.

Check for understanding before moving on.

Centering Exercise

Lead the children in a new centering exercise, "The Rainbow."

> Close your eyes and imagine that you're asleep and dreaming. In your dream, you can fly. You soar way, way up into the sky, and you decide to land on a white, fluffy cloud. You lie back and relax on that cloud as it floats lazily across the deep blue sky. You feel safe and warm. You look down and see other clouds below you. Far beneath those clouds is the world. It looks very small.
>
> You reach into your pocket and pull out all your worries and sadness. You drop them one at a time on the clouds that float below you, one worry, one sadness per cloud. Soon, the clouds change your worries and sadness into rain that falls gently to the ground. The rain washes away all the dust and dirt and reaches deep into the earth to help the plants and trees to grow.
>
> As the rain stops, you turn to see a beautiful rainbow. You float over on your cloud and sit on top of the rainbow. You smile to yourself because you know that *you* made that beautiful rainbow. Rainbows can only come *after* a rain. Without your worries and sadness, the clouds couldn't have made the rain. And there would be no beautiful rainbow now.
>
> You think to yourself, "You can never have a rainbow unless you first have a cloud and a storm."
>
> You're going to have a good day today. You're sitting on top of a rainbow!

Feelings Check-in

Do a feelings check-in with the children. Have them take their crayons and Feeling Wheels out of their folders. Direct the children to color in the section on the wheel that shows how they're feeling today. For younger children, read the names of the feelings on the wheel aloud (Angry [red], Scared [purple], Sad [blue], Glad [yellow]). The children can color in more than one feeling, since it's possible to have more than one feeling at a time. Tell the children that if they're having a feeling that is not named on the wheel, they can add a bubble to the outside of the wheel in any color they choose. Also point out that if they need to, the children can re-color a space.

When the children finish coloring, have a go-around, beginning with yourself. Invite each child to say his or her name and to show with the wheel how he or she is feeling. Be sure to accept each child's feeling(s) and to affirm each child. Ask the children to return the wheels to their folders.

Basic Facts Review

To help the children review the basic facts learned so far, show them Basic Facts Posters 1-17:

1. Chemical dependence is a <u>DISEASE</u>.

2. Alcohol and other drugs affect how people <u>ACT</u>, <u>THINK</u>, and <u>FEEL</u>, and how people TREAT you.

3. People with chemical dependence can't be cured, but they can get <u>BETTER</u>.

4. People can do things to feel <u>BETTER</u> without using alcohol or other drugs.

5. Children usually <u>LOVE</u> their parents, but since alcohol and other drugs affect how people act, think, feel, and treat you, children may not like how their parent <u>BEHAVES</u> when the parent uses alcohol or other drugs.

6. When someone is chemically dependent, it's nobody's <u>FAULT</u>.

7. The three **C**s are:

    1. Children don't <u>CAUSE</u> a parent to develop chemical dependence.

    2. Children can't <u>CONTROL</u> their parent's chemical dependence.

    3. Children can't <u>CURE</u> their parent's chemical dependence.

8. Children from chemically dependent families can:

    1. <u>LEARN</u> the facts about alcohol and other drugs.

    2. Ask for <u>HELP</u> for themselves.

    3. <u>RECOGNIZE</u>, <u>ACCEPT</u>, and <u>SHARE</u> their feelings.

9. Feelings aren't good or bad, or right or wrong; they just <u>ARE</u>.

10. Instead of swallowing feelings, it's better to <u>RECOGNIZE</u> them, <u>ACCEPT</u> them, and <u>SHARE</u> them with someone you trust.

11. When children are angry about a problem they can change, they should <u>USE</u> their anger to give them the power to make changes in themselves.

12. When children are angry about a problem they can't change, they should:

    1. <u>ACCEPT</u> what they can't change.

    2. <u>EXPRESS</u> their anger so they can let it <u>GO</u>.

    3. Do something <u>GOOD</u> for themselves.

13. Anger management is a way to <u>COPE</u> with anger.

14. The anger management steps are:

    1. <u>RECOGNIZE</u> that you're angry.

    2. <u>ACCEPT</u> your anger.

    3. <u>PRACTICE</u> some <u>RELAXATION</u>.

    4. <u>THINK</u> about ways to express the anger.

    5. <u>EVALUATE</u> the consequences.

    6. <u>CHOOSE</u> the best way.

    7. <u>EXPRESS</u> the anger in a helpful way.

15. Children can't <u>FIX</u> their parent's problems.

16. Children can take <u>GOOD CARE</u> of themselves.

17. Children should <u>WAIT</u> until a chemically dependent parent is sober before talking about how they feel.

In a go-around, ask a student to read the first fact aloud and to explain what it means. If a child has trouble, don't contradict or judge, simply clarify the explanation. Then ask all the children to repeat the fact together. Repeat the process for each fact.

Exploring the Story

The Story

Have the children settle themselves to hear the story. If you wish, let them hold their Peter the Puppy and Mrs. Owl puppets as they listen. Use the Peter the Puppy and Mrs. Owl toys to tell the story.

Hi, guys! Since I saw you last, I've been working hard on handling my feelings, solving my problems, and finding strategies to cope with the problems I can't solve. I hope you've been doing the same.

The first thing I do every day is remind myself that I can't cure my dad's chemical dependence. I also tell myself that I can't fix my parents' other problems, either. My parents are the only ones who can fix their problems. But I sort of wondered what Mrs. Owl meant when she said that I should take care of myself.

"Mrs. Owl," I asked, "when you said that I need to take good care of myself, did you mean that I should leave home and live by myself?"

"Oh, no, Peter," Mrs. Owl answered. "You're still a puppy, and you love your family. Your place is with them. When I said that you need to take good care of yourself, I meant that *you* can do things, even though you're still a puppy, that are good for you. You can take good care of your body, your mind, your feelings, and your choices. You can set goals to take care of yourself."

"Goals?" I asked. "Do you mean goals like in soccer or hockey or football?"

"No, not goals like that," laughed Mrs. Owl. "The goals I'm talking about are plans for things you can do for yourself. In fact, Peter," Mrs. Owl went on, "why don't you see if you can set some goals to do something good for your *whole self:* your body, your mind, your feelings, and your choices?"

So that's just what I did. I made a list called "Peter's Personal Goals." And here it is.

(If you made a poster showing Peter's Personal Goals, display it now. Then have Peter go through the goals one at a time.)

Peter's Personal Goals

For My Body:

1. Eat nutritious puppy food.
2. Get plenty of puppy exercise.
3. Get plenty of puppy sleep.

For My Mind:

1. Go to school every day, even if I'm worried.
2. Read every day.
3. Finish my homework every day.

For My Feelings:

1. Take time to have fun every day.

2. Make a new friend.

3. Find somebody like Mrs. Owl to talk to when I'm not at school.

For My Choices:

1. I will follow all the rules at school.

2. I will not use alcohol or other drugs.

Maybe you're wondering why I decided on my last goal, *I will not use alcohol or other drugs*. Well, I'll tell you. I decided not to use alcohol or other drugs—now and when I grow up—because Mrs. Owl told me that children and puppies who come from chemically dependent families are more likely to become chemically dependent than other children and puppies, UNLESS they make good decisions. I've seen how much the disease of chemical dependence can hurt everybody. So I decided that I'm going to take good care of myself and make the good choice *not* to use alcohol or other drugs.

I asked Mrs. Owl if she would see Milton and Crystal. I asked if she would help them set some goals. Mrs. Owl said sure she would, and so, she did.

Since Milton spends so much time working and studying, one of his goals is to take time to have fun every day. Because Crystal spends so much time by herself, one of her goals is to make a new friend. Also, both Milton and Crystal made the good choice *not* to use alcohol or other drugs.

You can make good choices, too. Maybe you can make a list of your personal goals to take good care of your body, mind, feelings, and choices. Maybe you can choose *not* to use alcohol or other drugs.

Discussion

Lead a discussion to help the children better understand the facts—the key concepts—presented in the story. Let them use their puppets when they speak; likewise, let them hold Peter the Puppy or Mrs. Owl. As they discuss, remember to go around the group, making sure that each child has an opportunity to add to the discussion. Encourage participation, but don't force it. Remember the group rule that allows a child to pass. Accept all ideas and answers, explaining or clarifying information where necessary to reinforce learning. To aid the discussion, you may use questions like the following:

- Can children cure a parent's chemical dependence? (No.)
- Can children fix their parents' other problems? (No.)

- Who *can* children take care of? (Themselves.)

- Does taking good care of themselves mean that children should leave home and live by themselves? (No. It means doing things that are good for them.)

- What are goals? (Goals are plans for things you'll do for yourself.)

- What goals did Peter make to take good care of his body? (To eat nutritious food, get plenty of exercise, and get plenty of sleep.)

- What goals did Peter make to take good care of his mind? (To go to school every day, read every day, and finish his homework each day.)

- What goals did Peter make to take good care of his feelings? (To have fun each day, make a new friend, find a trusted friend to talk to when he's not at school.)

- What are some other ways children can take care of their feelings? (Look for responses that indicate the children's awareness of their need to recognize, accept, and share their feelings, and express them appropriately.)

- What are some important choices that children have to make? (Expect answers such as whether to follow the rules at school and at home; whether to use alcohol or other drugs.)

Even if you choose not to use the above questions, make sure the discussion underscores these concepts.

Activity

Ask the children to retrieve their copies of Activity Sheet 10 and pencils. Read aloud the title at the top of the sheet: "My Personal Goals." The children will write two or three goals in each category to help them take care of their whole selves: body, mind, feelings, and choices. If you made a poster detailing Peter's goals, display it for the group to see.

Lead the children through the sections on the sheet, one at a time. Remind them of Peter's goals as they write their own. Make sure that everyone is finished with a section before moving on to the next. (Note: You may have to help the younger children write their goals.)

When the children finish the entire sheet, have a go-around. Invite each child to share his or her goals with the group. Take time to affirm the children on their goal setting and on their growing ability and willingness to take good care of themselves.

Give each child a sheet of stiff, colored construction paper and paste or a glue stick. Tell the children to center and then glue or paste Activity Sheet 10 onto the construction paper—making a "frame" for the sheet. Have the children put the sheets into their folders.

Basic Facts

Tell the children to take out Basic Facts Worksheet 9. Either read aloud the last two basic facts yourself, or have the children read them, one at a time.

18. Children from chemically dependent families are more likely to develop chemical dependence than are other children, unless they make GOOD DECISIONS.

19. Children need to take care of their BODIES, their FEELINGS, their MINDS, and their CHOICES.

Briefly discuss each fact, checking for understanding.

Give the children time to complete the bottom half of the worksheet by filling in the blanks. Then have the group read the facts aloud. Have the children put their worksheets in their folders, along with their Peter the Puppy and Mrs. Owl puppets.

Wrapping Up

Centering Exercise

Settle the children and then repeat "The Rainbow."

Affirmation

Involve the group in an affirmation. Stand and join in a circle with the children, holding hands. Go around and have the children share ways they can care for themselves. Begin the affirmation yourself: "One way I can take care of myself is. . . ."

Closing

Remain standing in a circle with the children, holding hands, and lead the group in the closing activity. Tell the children that you're going to make a *silent* wish for the child on your right. Then, when you've made the wish, *gently squeeze* the child's hand. The child makes a silent wish for the person on his or her right, then gently squeezes that child's hand, and so on. Continue around the circle until a wish and squeeze come back to you.

Collect the folders. Fill out a copy of the Process and Progress Form (see page 225) or the Progress Notes (see page 226) before leading the next session.

Note: If you've chosen to do the optional Session 10, before dismissing the children, explain that Session 10 will entail them making a presentation of the material they've learned so far. Tell the children how you plan to meet in order to practice for the presentation. Set up and confirm times with them.

Session 10: Group Presentation—Optional

Objectives

To help the children as individuals:

- demonstrate their understanding of the basic facts about chemical dependence
- grow in self esteem

To help the children as a group:

- share feelings of cohesiveness
- successfully complete a project

To help members of the audience:

- learn about chemical dependence
- become aware of some of the issues that arise from living in a family with chemical dependence
- recognize that help is available for those who live in a chemically dependent family

Session at a Glance

1. Group Rules: review—1 minute
2. Centering Exercise: an exercise chosen and led by the children—3 minutes
3. Feelings Check-in: color Feeling Wheel—5 minutes
4. Presentation: present all the basic facts—25 minutes
5. Audience Evaluation—3 minutes
6. Centering Exercise: repeat the chosen exercise—3 minutes
7. Affirmation: share what you liked or appreciated about the presentation—4 minutes
8. Closing: have a silent wish and squeeze—1 minute

Preparation

- Since the structure of this session varies from that of the other sessions, you may wish to schedule *two meeting times* to present it. Use the first time period as a practice session to help acquaint the children with the content of their presentation, to make all necessary preparations, and to practice it. Use the second time period to conduct the actual session, allowing the children to make their presentation.

- If you feel that using all eight steps as outlined in the "Session at a Glance" with an audience present would be too much or too difficult for the youngsters, use steps 1-3 with the children *alone;* then welcome in the audience for steps 4 (Presentation) and 5 (Audience Evaluation); finally, after the audience departs, do steps 6-8 with the children. You may, of course, include the audience in all eight steps of the session.

- Decide *in advance* on an appropriate audience to view the presentation. If this is the first time for such a presentation, you may wish to invite only the school principal or SAP staff.

- Make sure you have suitable seating arrangements for the audience.

- Have copies available of each of the nineteen Basic Facts Posters (see pages 201-219).

- Have the children's folders, with all their contents, available.

- If you wish, make the children copies of the presentation poem (see page 148), which they'll use throughout the presentation. *Note:* If you feel that the children will feel uncomfortable with the poem, you may choose *not* to include it.

- Display the posterboard copy of the group rules and the Peter the Puppy and Mrs. Owl toys.

- *Optional:* Clear a wall or bulletin board space in the meeting area where the children can post all nineteen Basic Facts Posters. Have pins or tape available for the children to post the posters.

- Have available the "Three Cs" poster (from Session 4) and the "Steps to Managing Anger" poster (from Sessions 7 and 8).

- Make copies of the Audience Evaluation Form (see page 221) and have pens or pencils available for audience members.

- Read through the session plan before meeting.

NOTES

Background and Guidelines

There's a lot to do for and in this session. Planning ahead, however, will make the task less daunting. The most effective way of guaranteeing the success of the children's presentation is advance planning and practice. Basically, the presentation entails the children presenting *all* the basic facts along with simple explanation to an invited audience. You need to decide who this audience will be and make arrangements to invite them well in advance.

Arrange to have one of the children lead the group and the audience in a centering exercise of the youngster's choice. The centering exercise will begin and help to conclude the session. If the children are too young to lead the exercise, plan on doing so yourself.

The children present the basic facts in eight sets. If possible, try to have at least two children present a set of facts. Thus, you'll need to designate eight pairs of children to present the sets. Since you don't have sixteen children in your group, pairs of children will need to be responsible for presenting more than one set of facts. In your practice session, you can assign the children to the different sets of facts.

Use the practice session to give the children copies of the presentation poem, which will serve as an introductory piece to each set of facts. Teach the poem, one line at a time. If possible, help the children learn it by heart. The poem remains the same throughout the presentation until the end, when the last line changes slightly (see page 152). Note this variation on the children's copies of the poem and draw their attention to it. Show the children the construction paper-backed copies of the Basic Facts Posters you made. For each fact the children are assigned, they'll display a poster of the fact, read it aloud, then tape or pin it in the space provided in the meeting room. Posting the posters should be optional.

After presenting a set of basic facts, the children will explain them to the audience by responding to questions from you, sharing posters from previous sessions, and, perhaps, by role playing. To help the presentation flow smoothly, have the children sit in the front row of the audience. Then, when you call on them to present their poem or set of facts, all they need do is stand, look at the audience, and speak slowly and distinctly. As you practice the presentation, the order and method should become clear to the children.

If your group and/or audience is made up of younger children, adjust, abbreviate, or simplify the presentation. Do your best, however, to see that all the basic facts are presented in some visual way: on a bulletin board, in handouts, or in poster form.

At the conclusion of the presentation, you will ask audience members to fill out an Audience Evaluation Form. The forms will give you important feedback and can serve as a referral source for future groups. If audience members, including teachers, identify themselves as children from chemically dependent families, be ready to refer them to available help—such is often the beginning of recovery.

The overall goal of the presentation is not to showcase group members' talents or academic abilities. Rather, the goal is to reinforce learning, to allow the group members to reach out to others, to convey a sense of hope to them, and to assure them that help *is* available to children from chemically dependent families.

Beginning the Session

Group Rules

Warmly welcome the children and their guests. Draw everyone's attention to the poster listing the group rules. Quickly review all the rules, calling on different children to read them one at a time.

1. I will keep what we talk about private. We call this confidentiality.
2. I will stay in my seat.
3. I will keep my hands to myself.
4. I will wait for my turn to talk, and I will listen carefully when others talk.
5. I won't tease or put other people down.
6. I can "pass" during go-arounds.
7. I will come to every group session.
8. I will make up any class work I miss.

Check that all present—including audience members—understand the group rules before moving on.

Centering Exercise

Explain to your guests that every time you meet, you always begin with a centering exercise to teach ways of relaxing and to help everyone get ready to work together. Then invite the designated child to lead the exercise.

Feelings Check-in

Give the children their folders. Have them take out their crayons and Feeling Wheels. Then do a feelings check-in with the children. Direct them to color in the section on the wheel that shows how they're feeling today. For younger children, read the names of the feelings on the wheel aloud (Angry [red], Scared [purple], Sad [blue], Glad [yellow]). The children can color in more than one feeling, since it's possible to have more than one feeling at a

147

time. If they're having a feeling that is not named on the wheel, they can add a bubble to the outside of the wheel in any color they choose. Also point out that if they need to, the children can re-color a space.

When the children finish coloring, have a go-around, beginning with yourself. Invite each child to show with the wheel how he or she is feeling. Be sure to accept each child's feeling(s) and to affirm each child. Ask the children to return the wheels to their folders.

Presentation

Introduction

With the toy Peter and Mrs. Owl at hand, introduce the presentation using the following or similar words: "We're part of the chemical dependence prevention program at (name of school). We've learned some important basic facts about alcohol and other drugs. We want to share some of what we've learned with you."

Presenting Basic Facts 1 and 2

Have the group recite the poem:

> *Chemical dependence is a scary disease*
> *That affects people's feelings and acts.*
> *Chemical dependence is a family disease,*
> *And it's time that we all learned the facts.*

Call on the children designated to present Basic Facts 1 and 2.

1. *Chemical dependence is a <u>DISEASE</u>.*
2. *Alcohol and other drugs affect how people <u>ACT</u>, <u>THINK</u>, and <u>FEEL</u>, and how people <u>TREAT</u> you.*

Have the children display a poster of each fact, read it aloud, and then post it.

Briefly explain Basic Fact 1 (the disease process) by saying something like the following: "We know that some people can use alcohol or other drugs and then stop. But when some other people use alcohol or other drugs, they can't stop! Using the drug makes some people lose choice and control over the drug. That means that they just can't say no. Instead, they want to take more and more of the drug. People like this have the disease called chemical dependence."

Expand on Basic Fact 2 by calling on group members to tell or show how alcohol and other drugs might make a person act, think, feel, and treat others.

Presenting Basic Facts 3 and 4

Move on to the next set of basic facts by having the group recite the poem. Then call on the children designated to present Basic Facts 3 and 4.

> 3. *People with chemical dependence cannot be cured, but they can get <u>BETTER</u>.*
>
> 4. *People can do things to feel <u>BETTER</u> without using alcohol or other drugs.*

Have the children display a poster of each fact, read it aloud, and then post it.

Help the children explain Basic Fact 3 by asking them to answer for the audience: "To get better, what two things do chemically dependent people have to do?" (First, see that they have a problem and decide they want to get better. Second, stop using alcohol and other drugs and change their ways of acting.)

Go on to tell the audience that people use alcohol or other drugs for a variety of reasons, but most often to help them change the way they *feel*. Then ask the children to tell what smart and safe things people could do to feel better *without* using alcohol or other drugs.

Presenting Basic Fact 5

To introduce the next basic fact, have the group recite the poem. Call on the children designated to present Basic Fact 5.

> 5. *Children usually <u>LOVE</u> their parents, but since alcohol and other drugs affect how people act, think, feel, and treat you, children may not like how their parent <u>BEHAVES</u> when the parent uses alcohol or other drugs.*

Have the children display a poster of the fact, read it aloud, and then post it.

To expand on Basic Fact 5, call on different children to name behaviors of a chemically dependent parent that a child may notice and dislike. Note that the children are not asked to reveal anything of their home life, only to give examples of behavior. As you conclude, point out to the audience how Basic Fact 5 reveals that children can love their parents and be angry with them at the same time, and that this can be very confusing for children.

Presenting Basic Facts 6, 7, and 8

Move on to the next set of basic facts by having the group recite the poem. Then call on the children designated to present Basic Facts 6, 7, and 8.

> 6. *When someone is chemically dependent, it's nobody's <u>FAULT</u>.*
>
> 7. *The three Cs are:*
>
>   *1. Children don't <u>CAUSE</u> a parent to develop chemical dependence.*
>
>   *2. Children can't <u>CONTROL</u> their parent's chemical dependence.*
>
>   *3. Children can't <u>CURE</u> their parent's chemical dependence.*

8. *Children from chemically dependent families can:*
   1. *LEARN the facts about alcohol and other drugs.*
   2. *Ask for HELP for themselves.*
   3. *RECOGNIZE, ACCEPT, and SHARE their feelings.*

Have the children display a poster of each fact, read it aloud, and then post it.

Tell the audience: "Children often believe that their family's problems are their fault, that they've *caused* a parent's chemical dependence: 'My mom uses drugs because I fight too much with my sister.' But this isn't the case. No one is at fault for a person's chemical dependence. *No one.* Some people just have it, like some people have the disease of diabetes. That's why it's important for children to learn the three Cs."

Display the poster with the three Cs (from Session 4). Point out to the audience that the three Cs are included in Basic Fact 7. Use the following questions to help the children explain the three Cs:

- What are some things children might think they do to *cause* a parent to develop chemical dependence? (Fighting at home, arguing with parents, or getting into trouble at school.)

- What are some things children might do to try to *control* a parent's chemical dependence? (Hide or destroy the alcohol or other drug; cover up or make excuses for the chemically dependent person.)

- What might children do to try and *cure* a parent's chemical dependence? (Tell a parent to go to the hospital; try to act and be perfect, thinking that their "improved" behavior will cure the disease.)

- Will any of these things work? (No.)

After the children respond to the questions, invite them to recite from memory the three Cs and the three steps children from chemically dependent families can take.

Presenting Basic Facts 9 and 10

Move on to the next set of basic facts by having the group recite the poem. Then call on the children designated to present Basic Facts 9 and 10.

9. *Feelings aren't good or bad, or right or wrong; they just ARE.*

10. *Instead of swallowing feelings, it's better to RECOGNIZE them, ACCEPT them, and SHARE them with someone you trust.*

Have the children display a poster of each of the facts, read it aloud, and then post it.

Point out to the audience that since everyone has feelings, and since chemical dependence is such a "feeling" disease, it's important for children to learn how to deal with their feelings.

Explain that recognizing feelings means being able to name them, accepting feelings means telling yourself it's okay to have them, and sharing feelings means being able to tell someone else *how* you feel.

Presenting Basic Facts 11, 12, 13, and 14

Move on to the next set of basic facts by having the group recite the poem. Then call on the children designated to present Basic Facts 11, 12, 13, and 14.

11. *When children are angry about a problem they can change, they should <u>USE</u> their anger to give them the power to make changes in themselves.*

12. *When children are angry about a problem they cannot change, they should:*

    1. <u>ACCEPT</u> what they cannot change.

    2. <u>EXPRESS</u> their anger so they can let it <u>GO</u>.

    3. Do something <u>GOOD</u> for themselves.

13. *Anger management is a way to <u>COPE</u> with anger.*

14. *The anger management steps are:*

    1. <u>RECOGNIZE</u> that you are angry.

    2. <u>ACCEPT</u> your anger.

    3. <u>PRACTICE</u> some <u>RELAXATION</u>.

    4. <u>THINK</u> about ways to express the anger.

    5. <u>EVALUATE</u> the consequences.

    6. <u>CHOOSE</u> the best way.

    7. <u>EXPRESS</u> the anger in a helpful way.

Have the children display a poster of each of the facts, read it aloud, and then post it.

Next, ask the children to display the poster entitled "Steps to Managing Anger" (from Session 7) that shows the seven paw prints. For the benefit of the audience, briefly go through the steps, using an appropriate example (see the story in Session 7) and asking the children if different ways to express anger are helpful or harmful.

Presenting Basic Facts 15, 16, and 17

Move on to the next set of basic facts by having the group recite the poem. Then call on the children designated to present Basic Facts 15, 16, and 17.

15. *Children cannot <u>FIX</u> their parents' problems.*

16. *Children can take <u>GOOD CARE</u> of themselves.*

17. *Children should WAIT until a chemically dependent parent is sober before talking about how they feel.*

Have the children display a poster of each of the facts, read it aloud, and then post it.

A good way to explain these facts to the audience is to have one of the children explain the third problem situation faced by Peter the Puppy on Activity Sheet 9 ("My dad promised to play fetch with me. Instead, he's asleep on the couch from drinking too much alcohol"). Then either have children read aloud a coping strategy for Peter from Activity Sheet 9, or, if time allows, have a few of the children role-play the coping strategy.

Conclude the explanation of these facts in words similar to the following: "It's important to remember how alcohol and other drugs affect the way people think. Since a chemically dependent person's thinking is affected, children should wait until the effects of the alcohol or other drug wear off before talking about anything important with the person."

Presenting Basic Facts 18 and 19

Move on to the final two basic facts by having the group recite the poem. Then call on the children designated to present Basic Facts 18 and 19.

18. *Children from chemically dependent families are more likely to develop chemical dependence than are other children, unless they make GOOD DECISIONS.*

19. *Children need to take care of their BODIES, their FEELINGS, their MINDS, and their CHOICES.*

Have the children display a poster of each of the facts, read it aloud, and then post it.

Explain to the audience that children from chemically dependent families are statistically at greater risk to develop chemical dependence themselves, but they can live healthy lives if they learn to make good decisions. A very good decision that these children can make is *never to use alcohol or other drugs* (the no-use rule).

Concluding the Presentation

Conclude the presentation by having the group stand, face the audience, and recite the poem, but with a new final line:

> *Chemical dependence is a scary disease*
> *That affects people's feelings and acts.*
> *Chemical dependence is a family disease,*
> *And we thank you for hearing the facts.*

Have the children take a bow. Lead the audience in applause.

Wrapping Up

Audience Evaluation

Pass out copies of the Audience Evaluation Form and pens or pencils to audience members. Encourage them to spend a moment completing the form. When audience members finish writing, collect the forms, pens, and pencils.

Centering Exercise

Ask the child who led the centering exercise at the beginning of the session to repeat it.

Affirmation

Afterward, involve group and audience members in an affirmation. Invite everyone to stand in a circle and hold hands. Go around and have everyone share something he or she liked or appreciated about the group's presentation. Begin the affirmation yourself: "One thing I really liked about the presentation was...."

Closing

Remain in the circle with everyone holding hands and lead the closing activity. Explain that you're going to make a *silent* wish for the person on your right. Then, when you've made the wish, *gently squeeze* the person's hand. The individual makes a silent wish for the person on his or her right, then gently squeezes that person's hand, and so on. Continue around the circle until a wish and squeeze come back to you.

Thank the audience for their participation. Let the group members know that you are looking forward to seeing them at your next session.

Collect the children's folders. Fill out a copy of the Process and Progress Form (see page 225) or the Progress Notes (see page 226) before leading the next session.

Session 11: Peter Says Goodbye

Objectives

To help the children:

- review all the basic facts about chemical dependence
- create a personal support system
- close out their group experience

Session at a Glance

1. Group Rules: review—1 minute
2. Centering Exercise: "The Waterfall"—2 minutes
3. Feelings Check-in: color Feeling Wheel—5 minutes
4. Basic Facts Review (Optional: Process Session 10's Presentation)—8 minutes
5. The Story—4 minutes
6. Discussion—3 minutes
7. Activity: make a booklet of people who can offer support (Activity Sheet 11)—7 minutes
8. Group Evaluation—4 minutes
9. Certificates and Awards—4 minutes
10. Affirmation and Refreshments: tell what you liked best about group and share refreshments—6 minutes
11. Closing: have a silent wish and squeeze—1 minute

Preparation

- Display the posterboard copy of the group rules.

- Have the toy Peter the Puppy, the toy Mrs. Owl, and Basic Facts Posters 1-19 available.

- Make each child a copy of All the Basic Facts (see page 220). Center and glue or paste each sheet on a piece of colored construction paper.

- Make sure the children's folders contain the Feeling Wheel and pencils and crayons (including red, purple, blue, and yellow); then add the following materials to each folder:

  - a copy of Activity Sheet 11 ("My Personal Yellow Pages")

  - a copy of All the Basic Facts mounted on construction paper (see above)

- Optional: Make a poster of Peter the Puppy's "My Personal Yellow Pages" (see the story, page 162) to use with the children during the story.

- Use a copy of Activity Sheet 11 to make a sample "My Personal Yellow Pages" booklet for the children to use as a model.

- To help the children complete their personal yellow pages, have ready a brief list of emergency phone numbers and the numbers of local self-help or crisis agencies that deal with chemical dependence, for example, AA, Alanon, and Alateen.

- Make copies of the Group Evaluation Form (see page 222).

- Make copies of the Group Certificate (see page 223). Complete a certificate for each group member by filling in the child's name on the line provided.

- Make each child a simple Group Award Badge (see page 224, for a sample and directions).

- Make arrangements to serve refreshments during the wrapping-up activity. The children may enjoy fruit and juice or cookies and milk. Home-made cookies cut in the shape of dog biscuits would be a big hit.

- Read through the session plan before meeting.

NOTES

Background and Guidelines

This session summarizes the themes of the group curriculum: education about alcohol and other drugs, correcting misconceptions, identifying and accepting feelings, and empowerment. The children review all the basic facts and evaluate their group experience.

Over the course of the group process, the children discovered that although they can't cure the chemical dependence in their family or fix family problems, they can do some crucial things to help themselves. In this session, the children realize something new: they don't have to be alone as they focus on themselves. They see that not only is it okay to ask for help, but also it's healthy and smart. Children can ask for help to learn how to deal with their feelings, how to develop coping strategies, and how to learn new skills. Thus, although this session marks the end of their group experience, it helps the children see that their support system is not diminishing, but has grown and can continue to expand.

As leader, you can help the children see that the average person needs a support system of about thirty people, not just two or three. Children need to understand that they can ask for help in many different areas of their lives, and that it's perfectly okay to have different people help in different ways at different times.

The session provides the children with a number of opportunities to share what they've gained and will remember from their group experience. But, as the children leave the group, the session does more than give them an opportunity to review. Through the story, the children discover that despite all they've learned, things will happen in the future that will upset them; that's why a support system is so vital. Emphasize this important point, stressing that using their support system (their "personal yellow pages" and other sources of help) during upsetting times is a wonderful way for the children to take good care of themselves.

Note that the centering exercise is not repeated in this final session. In its place is a small ceremony where the children receive certificates and awards for taking part in the Peter the Puppy Group. Be sure to have the certificates and award badges ready for the children. If possible, provide some refreshments. This not only helps the children feel self-worth, but also it tells them that they should and can have some fun, that they should and can celebrate their learning.

Sometimes, the end of group sessions is a bittersweet time for children. Be ready for some of this. Don't be afraid to speak and show your appreciation for and feelings toward the children.

Beginning the Session

Group Rules

Welcome the children warmly, pass out folders, and draw attention to the poster listing the group rules. Quickly review all the rules, calling on different children to read them one at a time.

1. I will keep what we talk about private. We call this confidentiality.
2. I will stay in my seat.
3. I will keep my hands to myself.
4. I will wait for my turn to talk, and I will listen carefully when others talk.
5. I won't tease or put other people down.
6. I can "pass" during go-arounds.
7. I will come to every group session.
8. I will make up any class work I miss.

Tell the youngsters that these are good rules for them to use in other group situations. With some adaptation, they would work well in their classrooms or at home. Thank the children for doing a good job of sticking to their rules throughout the group sessions.

Centering Exercise

Lead the children in the centering exercise, "The Waterfall."

> Close your eyes and relax. Pretend that you're walking on a beautiful path in the mountains. You're taking a hike down the mountain. It's October, and the sky is clear and a deep shade of blue. The air is cool, but the sun is warm. The leaves are changing colors. Look at the beautiful shades of red, orange, and yellow. Imagine what the orange and yellow leaves look like as you look up and see them like lace against the sky.
>
> You keep walking down the mountain path until you come upon a waterfall, a beautiful cascading waterfall, a stream tumbling down over huge boulders. You sit on a boulder near the waterfall, and you empty your mind. You pay attention to the sound of the water as it rushes over the boulders and trickles down the stream. You imagine that the water is rushing over you and making you feel clean and refreshed.
>
> As you sit quietly on the boulder, you drink in the warmth of the sun. You see leaves that have fallen into the stream. They float like tiny boats on the bubbling water.

You decide to put all your worries, problems, and frustrations on the leaves and to let them all float away.

So if you're worried because *(use appropriate examples specific to the children in your group, such as . . .)* you don't have some homework that's due today, let that worry float away on a leaf. Or, if you had a fight on the bus this morning, and you're afraid you might get suspended, put that worry on a leaf and let it float away. Or, if you feel angry over your mom's yelling at you because she didn't like the outfit you put on this morning, put that anger on a leaf and watch it float away.

Put all your worries, problems, and frustrations on leaves and watch them all float away. Soon they're all gone. When you open your eyes, you're going to be able to work hard because all your problems have floated away. You can go back and solve these problems later.

Feelings Check-in

Do a feelings check-in with the children. Have them take their crayons and Feeling Wheels out of their folders. Direct the children to color in the section on the wheel that shows how they're feeling today. For younger children, read the names of the feelings on the wheel aloud (Angry [red], Scared [purple], Sad [blue], Glad [yellow]). The children can color in more than one feeling, since it's possible to have more than one feeling at a time. Tell the children that if they're having a feeling that is not named on the wheel, they can add a bubble to the outside of the wheel in any color they choose. Also point out that if they need to, the children can re-color a space.

When the children finish coloring, have a go-around, beginning with yourself. Invite each child to say his or her name and to show with the wheel how he or she is feeling. Be sure to accept each child's feeling(s) and to affirm each child. Ask the children to return the wheels to their folders.

Basic Facts Review

To help the children review all the basic facts, have the youngsters retrieve their mounted copies of All the Basic Facts from their folders. Explain that they can keep this list to remind them of the many things they've learned about chemical dependence. You may also use copies of Basic Facts Posters 1-19 in the review.

1. Chemical dependence is a <u>DISEASE</u>.

2. Alcohol and other drugs affect how people <u>ACT</u>, <u>THINK</u>, and <u>FEEL</u>, and how people TREAT you.

3. People with chemical dependence can't be cured, but they can get <u>BETTER</u>.

4. People can do things to feel <u>BETTER</u> without using alcohol or other drugs.

5. Children usually <u>LOVE</u> their parents, but since alcohol and other drugs affect how people act, think, feel, and treat you, children may not like how their parent <u>BEHAVES</u> when the parent uses alcohol or other drugs.

6. When someone is chemically dependent, it's nobody's <u>FAULT</u>.

7. The three **Cs** are:

    1. Children don't <u>CAUSE</u> a parent to develop chemical dependence.

    2. Children can't <u>CONTROL</u> their parent's chemical dependence.

    3. Children can't <u>CURE</u> their parent's chemical dependence.

8. Children from chemically dependent families can:

    1. <u>LEARN</u> the facts about alcohol and other drugs.

    2. Ask for <u>HELP</u> for themselves.

    3. <u>RECOGNIZE</u>, <u>ACCEPT</u>, and <u>SHARE</u> their feelings.

9. Feelings aren't good or bad, or right or wrong; they just <u>ARE</u>.

10. Instead of swallowing feelings, it's better to <u>RECOGNIZE</u> them, <u>ACCEPT</u> them, and <u>SHARE</u> them with someone you trust.

11. When children are angry about a problem they can change, they should <u>USE</u> their anger to give them the power to make changes in themselves.

12. When children are angry about a problem they can't change, they should:

    1. <u>ACCEPT</u> what they can't change.

    2. <u>EXPRESS</u> their anger so they can let it <u>GO</u>.

    3. Do something <u>GOOD</u> for themselves.

13. Anger management is a way to <u>COPE</u> with anger.

14. The anger management steps are:

    1. <u>RECOGNIZE</u> that you're angry.

    2. <u>ACCEPT</u> your anger.

    3. <u>PRACTICE</u> some <u>RELAXATION</u>.

    4. <u>THINK</u> about ways to express the anger.

    5. <u>EVALUATE</u> the consequences.

    6. <u>CHOOSE</u> the best way.

    7. <u>EXPRESS</u> the anger in a helpful way.

15. Children can't <u>FIX</u> their parent's problems.
16. Children can take <u>GOOD CARE</u> of themselves.
17. Children should <u>WAIT</u> until a chemically dependent parent is sober before talking about how they feel.
18. Children from chemically dependent families are more likely to develop chemical dependence than are other children, unless they make <u>GOOD DECISIONS.</u>
19. Children need to take care of their <u>BODIES</u>, their <u>FEELINGS,</u> their <u>MINDS</u>, and their <u>CHOICES</u>.

In a go-around, ask a student to read the first fact aloud and to explain what it means. If a child has trouble, don't contradict or judge, simply clarify the explanation. Then ask all the children to repeat the fact together. Repeat the process for each fact.

Optional: If the group took part in the Presentation of Session 10, take a moment to process it with the children. Ask them what was hard and easy about the presentation, what was the most fun, what could have made it better. Record the children's observations to use and consider when presenting Session 10 in the future.

Exploring the Story

The Story

Have the children settle themselves to hear the story. If you wish, let them hold their Peter the Puppy and Mrs. Owl puppets as they listen. Use the Peter the Puppy and Mrs. Owl toys to tell the story.

> It's hard to believe that our time together as a group is almost finished. So before we're done, I want you to know how much you've helped me learn. I feel proud of the changes I've made. I know that I had some wrong ideas before, but now I know the facts about chemical dependence. I know it's important for me to ask for help. And I know that you and I have become friends.
>
> Can you remember when we first met? Back then I used to bite other puppies and get into trouble all the time. As a matter of fact, I came close to biting you a couple of times! I was that way because I swallowed my feelings until they just exploded out of me. Now I recognize my feelings, and I know how to relax through exercises like "Breathing Through My Feet," "The Space Shuttle," and "The Waterfall."
>
> I used to be so angry all the time. Now I use my anger to work for me. If I feel angry about having a lot of homework, I use my anger to give me the power to get me started. Or, I express my anger so I can let it go—I run into my room and punch my pillow.

I don't get into so much trouble anymore. And let me tell you, I feel very happy about that.

Things at home haven't changed much. My dad still uses alcohol, and I'm still worried about his chemical dependence. But now I know that chemical dependence is a disease that's not my fault. I know I didn't cause it. I know I can't control it. I know I can't cure it. But I also know that I can do things to help myself and take good care of myself, so that I can grow up to be a strong and healthy dog.

Mrs. Owl is proud of me and the changes I've made. She's happy that I'm doing so much better. But she told me that not everything will always be perfect.

"Peter," she said, "sometimes things in your life will bother you. That's the way life is. But, in tough times, you can always turn to others for help. Remember, you don't have to solve all your problems by yourself. You don't even have to figure out how to cope with your problems all by yourself."

"Do you mean if I have a problem with a question on a test in school that it would be okay to ask someone for the answer?" I asked.

"No, Peter," Mrs. Owl answered. "When you're taking a test in school, it's not okay to ask someone else for help, but it is okay to ask someone for help in solving a homework problem. It's also okay to ask a friend to listen when you have a difficult feeling to share. And it's very much okay to have a friend to play with to make sure that you have fun every day."

"But, Mrs. Owl, who will I call if I need help?" I asked. "I know I have you for a friend, but where else can I look for help? Who else can I call?"

"Ah ha!" Mrs. Owl exclaimed. "You've given me a great idea, Peter. When grown-ups need help and don't know who to call, they look in the yellow pages of the telephone book. I think you should make your own yellow pages of people you can call or go to for help whenever you're having trouble."

So that's what I did. I made my own special list of people I could call for help. I call it My Personal Yellow Pages.

(Show the children the poster "My Personal Yellow Pages," outlining Peter's list of people to call for help. Have Peter go through the list with the group.)

My Personal Yellow Pages

People to have fun with:

Thomas Barker, Patty Poodle, and the Labrador twins, Matthew and Leigh

People to ask for help with schoolwork:

My teacher, the librarian, Dad (if he's not using alcohol or other drugs), Milton or Thomas Barker (because they're real good at schoolwork)

People to talk to when I have a problem or feel sad or angry:

Mom (if she's not upset); my toy boy, Harvey; Mrs. Owl; and Uncle Jack Spaniel

Important phone numbers:

Emergency: 911

Alcoholics Anonymous: 555-1000

Alanon: 555-2000

Alateen: 555-3000

That's my personal yellow pages. Maybe you can make your own. Then you would know who to call or go to whenever you're in trouble and need help.

Right now, I want to thank you for *your* help. When I first met you, I wasn't feeling very well. But telling you about my family and my dad's chemical dependence has helped me understand it. Because of the facts we've learned and friendship we've shared, I'm feeling much better now.

I hope you've learned ways to be a healthier, happier puppy—Whoops! I mean person—especially if you live in a family where there's chemical dependence.

I suppose there are lots of different things I could say to you. But I think the best thing I can say is

Good Luck and Goodbye.

Discussion

Lead a discussion to help the children better understand the facts—the key concepts—presented in the story. Let them use their puppets when they speak, or let them hold Peter the Puppy or Mrs. Owl. As they discuss, remember to go around the group, making sure that each child has an opportunity to add to the discussion. Encourage participation, but don't force it. Remember the group rule that allows a child to pass. Accept all ideas and answers, explaining or clarifying information where necessary to reinforce learning. To aid the discussion, you may use questions like the following:

- How has Peter changed through his work with Mrs. Owl? (Look for answers such as: he has learned the facts about chemical dependence; he has stopped biting other puppies.)

- What coping strategies does Peter use now? (He recognizes and shares his feelings; he uses centering exercises; he remembers that he didn't cause and can't control or cure his dad's chemical dependence.)

- Do you think that Peter's troubles are over, that life will be perfect for him from now on? (No, that's not the way life is.)

- Is it okay to ask other people for help? (Yes. It's okay to have friends to have fun with; to ask for help with schoolwork; to have people to talk to when you have a problem or are feeling sad or angry.)

Even if you choose not to use the above questions, make sure the discussion underscores these concepts. Thank the children for taking part in the discussion. Affirm how much they've learned.

Activity

Ask the children to retrieve their copies of Activity Sheet 11. Display the sample yellow pages booklet you made prior to the session. Show the group how to fold the sheet to make their own booklets. Have the children write their names on the line at the top of the booklet's cover page. Read aloud the title on the cover, "My Personal Yellow Pages." Then go through the booklet page by page. For each page, read the heading, then give the children time to complete the page.

For the last page, "Important phone numbers," you may have to offer some assistance. For example, since most communities have 911 service, 911 is *the* emergency telephone number. If, however, there is no 911 service in your area, direct the children to write in "O" for Operator or your specific, local emergency number. You might want to make available the numbers of local chemical dependence hotlines and the numbers for Alcoholics Anonymous, Alanon, or Alateen, explaining that there are caring people at these numbers who can listen and offer help.

When the children finish writing, have a go-around. Invite each child to share from his or her yellow pages. Have the children place their yellow pages in their folders. Tell them they may take their folders home with them.

Group Evaluation

Since the children have completed all the basic facts, there is no Basic Facts Worksheet for this session. Instead, pass out copies of the Group Evaluation Form and ask the children to complete it. Explain to the youngsters that their honesty will help you make the group better for other children. Point out that they need not put their names on the form. Older children may work on their own. Younger children, however, may require your assistance. For example, you may have to read each question aloud, or you may have to help with writing or spelling. When the children finish, collect the forms to use when you evaluate the group program.

Wrapping Up

Certificates and Awards

Thank the children for their hard work, sharing, and openness by calling each child forward and presenting him or her with a Group Certificate and an award badge. As you present the certificates and badges, offer a personal note of thanks, mentioning something special to each child about his or her unique contribution to the group.

Affirmation and Refreshments

Involve the group in a final affirmation. Stand and join in a circle with the children, holding hands. Go around and have the children share something that they really liked about the group. Begin the affirmation yourself: "What I liked most about this group is...." After everyone has had a chance to share, surprise the children with some refreshments. (Try those cookie dog biscuits!)

Closing

Lead the group in the closing activity: Stand and join in a circle with the children, holding hands. Tell the children that you're going to make a *silent* wish for the child on your right. Then, when you've made the wish, *gently squeeze* the child's hand. The child makes a silent wish for the person on his or her right, then gently squeezes that child's hand, and so on. Continue around the circle until a wish and squeeze come back to you.

Say a personal goodbye to the children.

Fill out a copy of the Process and Progress Form (see page 225) or the Progress Notes (see page 226).

Part Three

Support Materials

This section of the manual includes the tools you'll need to develop and support the group program in your school. Each of the following materials is printed in blackline master form and is suitable for copying on most photocopy machines.

Group Rules Contract. You'll need a copy of this contract for every group member. The Group Rules Contract will be used in Session 1 and in the screening interview.

Feeling Wheel. This sheet will aid you in doing a feelings check-in with the children. Each group member will need one copy. The children will use their copy of the Feeling Wheel in Sessions 2-11.

Activity Sheets. There are eleven Activity Sheets. They'll be used in the various sessions. Make sure that everyone in your group has a copy of the sheet(s) needed. It's a good idea to make extra copies in case children have problems.

Basic Facts Worksheets. The nine Basic Facts Worksheets will be used by the children in their sessions together.

Basic Facts Worksheets with Answers Dotted In. These nine worksheets have the answers dotted in to help younger group members (K-first grade) and special education populations.

Basic Facts Posters. These nineteen sheets reproduce the basic facts in large print. They can be photocopied and laminated for use in the sessions. They also can be made into transparencies for larger presentations.

All the Basic Facts. The complete list of basic facts is to be copied and mounted on construction paper and given out in Session 11.

Audience Evaluation Form. This form may be used to evaluate the optional children's presentation in Session 10. It is designed to provide important feedback regarding the presentation's effectiveness and to serve as a referral source for future groups.

Group Evaluation Form. This form is to be used in Session 11 by the children to evaluate their total group experience.

Group Certificate. This award or participation certificate may be photocopied, filled out, and given to each group member during Session 11.

Group Award Badge. This sheet provides a pattern and the directions for making the children award badges, which are presented in Session 11.

Process and Progress Form. This form is for you, the group leader. Make eleven copies of the form. After each session, fill out a copy of the form in order to evaluate the session and to keep timely notes on the progress of the group.

Progress Notes. This two-page form is a more condensed version of the Process and Progress Form and is suitable for the more experienced group leader. Simply copy each page and fill out the appropriate section after each group session.

Self-Referral Group Survey Form. Designed for children grades 2 and up, this form should be made available to children after they've heard about the purpose of the support groups. Use the form in conjunction with a presentation at which available groups are explained to the children (see pages 17-18). When the children fill out the form, explain that if they want to be in more than one group, they should number their choices in priority. Also, make sure the children know that not everyone may be in groups right away and that groups will be offered according to need and time.

Parental Consent Letter. Once children have been referred or self-referred to a group, you should seek parental consent by sending parents a copy of a letter like the one provided here.

Screening Interview Outline. After referrals are obtained and categorized, the children need to be interviewed individually. The Screening Interview Outline will help you get basic, necessary information about the children and their daily life. If children seem like appropriate candidates, be sure to explain the group format and to show them a copy of the Group Rules Contract.

This section of the manual also includes a list of professional resources for your enrichment and names and addresses of helping agencies.

Group Rules Contract

1. I will keep what we talk about private.
   We call this confidentiality.

2. I will stay in my seat.

3. I will keep my hands to myself.

4. I will wait for my turn to talk,
   and I will listen carefully when others talk.

5. I won't tease or put other people down.

6. I can "pass" during go-arounds.

7. I will come to every group session.

8. I will make up any class work I miss.

_____
Name

_____
Date

Feeling Wheel

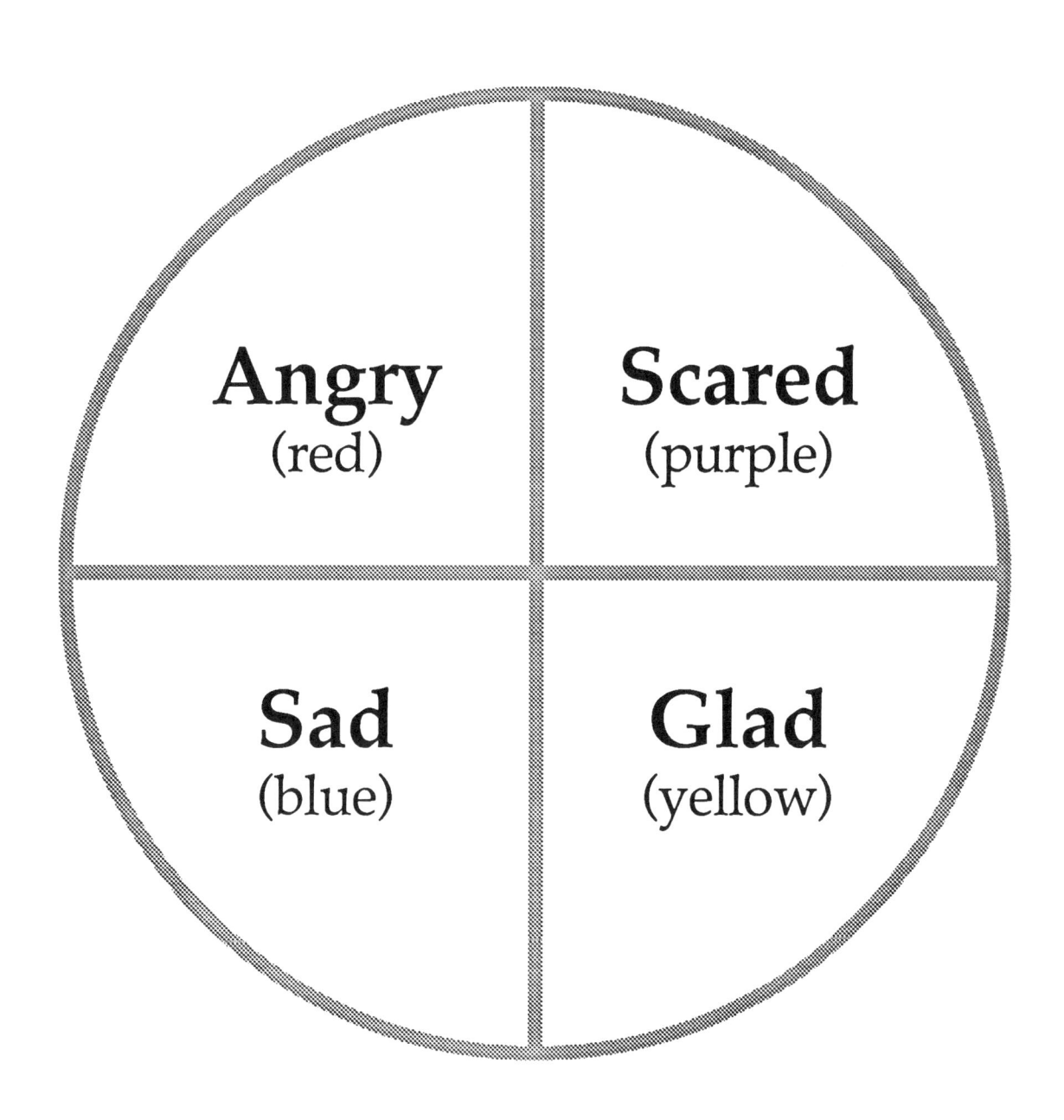

Angry (red)	**Scared** (purple)
Sad (blue)	**Glad** (yellow)

Activity Sheet 1

Peter the Puppy Puppet

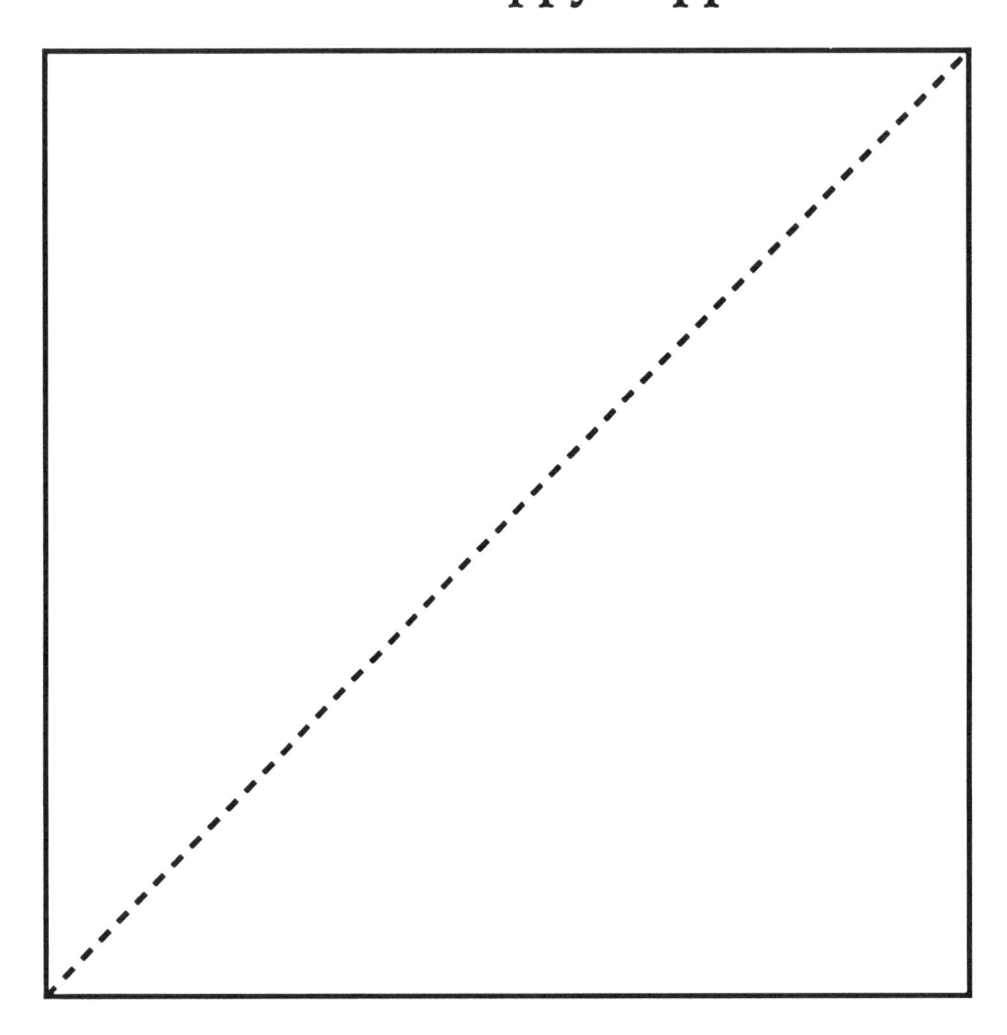

1. Cut out the square.
2. Fold on the dotted line.
3. Fold edges down to make puppy ears.
4. Draw mouth, nose, and eyes that show any feeling you wish.

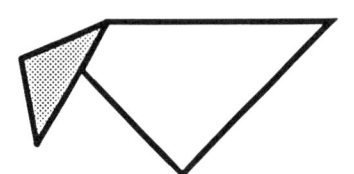

Activity Sheet 2

This person has had too much alcohol to drink or has taken too many other drugs.

Activity Sheet 3

I Feel Better When I...

Activity Sheet 4
A Feeling Picture of My Family

Draw a picture that shows everyone in your family.
Color each person the feeling he or she has most often.

Red = Angry   Blue = Sad   Yellow = Glad   Purple = Scared

Activity Sheet 5
Mrs. Owl Puppet

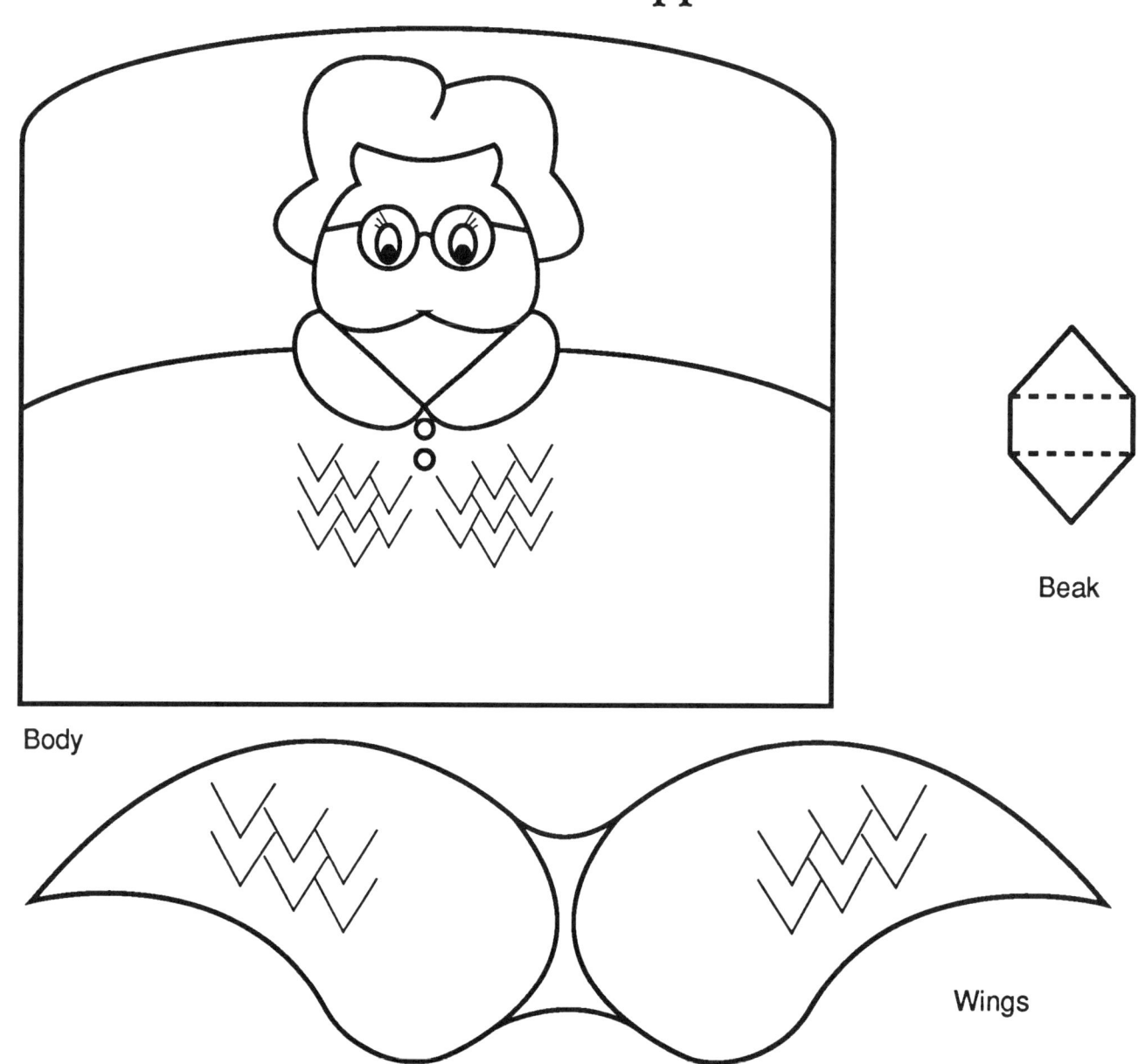

Beak

Body

Wings

1. Color Mrs. Owl with your favorite colors. Color her beak, her body, and her wings.
2. Cut out the body. Print your name on the back.
   Roll the ends toward the back and tape or paste together.
3. Cut out the beak. Tape or paste the beak onto Mrs. Owl's face.
4. Cut out the wings. Tape or paste them onto Mrs. Owl's back.

Activity Sheet 6
Feelings

Read each sentence. Color in the "feeling" you have about what the sentence says in the space provided.

Red = Angry   Blue = Sad   Yellow = Glad   Purple = Scared

1. When someone tells me to go to bed at night, I feel

2. When I have to get ready for school, I feel

3. When people in my family argue, I feel

4. When I'm sitting in class at school, I feel

5. If people in my house drank too much or used other drugs, I might feel

6. Going places with my family makes me feel

7. Fighting with a friend makes me feel

8. When I have to go home each day after school, I feel

Activity Sheet 7

Anger at Work

Draw a picture of a way you can make your anger work for you, or a way you can use your anger to make changes in yourself. Write if you don't want to draw.

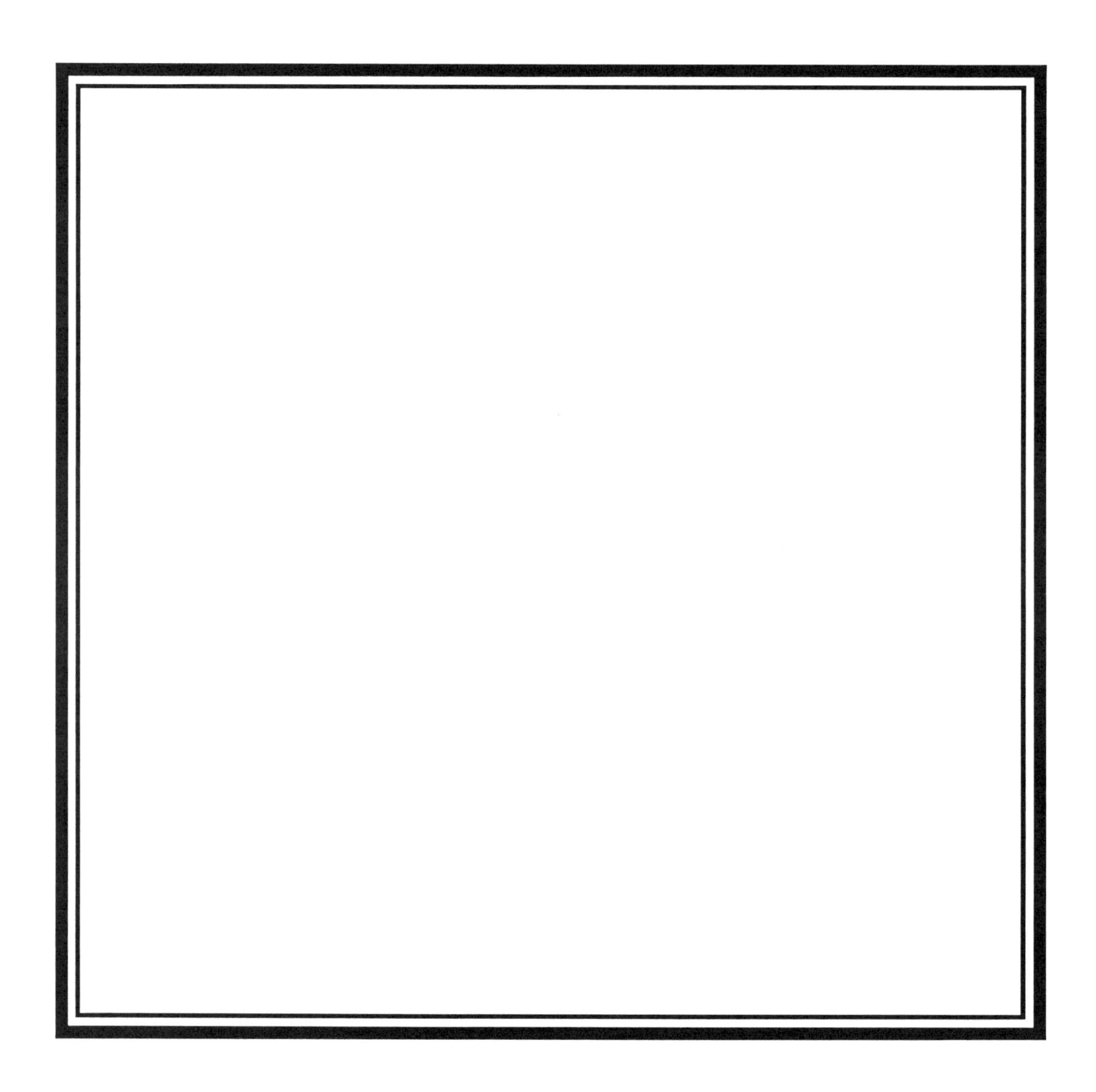

Activity Sheet 8
Helpful Ways I Can Express Anger

RECOGNIZE

ACCEPT

RELAX

THINK

EVALUATE

CHOOSE

EXPRESS

Activity Sheet 9
Coping Strategies

Problem Situation 1

My mom and dad are having a really bad fight
and throwing things at each other.

Coping Strategy

_____

_____

Problem Situation 2

My mom is crying because it's late and my dad hasn't come home.

Coping Strategy

_____

_____

Problem Situation 3

My dad promised to play fetch with me.
Instead, he's asleep on the couch from drinking too much alcohol.

Coping Strategy

_____

_____

Activity Sheet 10
My Personal Goals

For My Body:

_____
_____
_____
_____

For My Mind:

_____
_____
_____
_____

For My Feelings:

_____
_____
_____
_____

For My Choices:

_____
_____
_____
_____

Activity Sheet 11

People to talk to when I have a problem or feel sad or angry:

_____
_____
_____
_____
_____

Important phone numbers:

Emergency: _____
_____
_____
_____
_____

People to ask for help with schoolwork:

_____
_____
_____
_____
_____

My Personal Yellow Pages
People to have fun with:

_____
_____
_____
_____
_____

Basic Facts Worksheet 1

1. Chemical dependence is a <u>DISEASE</u>.

2. Alcohol and other drugs affect how people <u>ACT</u>, <u>THINK</u>, and <u>FEEL</u>, and how people <u>TREAT</u> you.

Practice

1. Chemical dependence is a _____ .

2. Alcohol and other drugs affect how people _____, _____, and _____, and how people _____ you.

Basic Facts Worksheet 2

3. People with chemical dependence can't be cured, but they can get <u>BETTER</u>.

4. People can do things to feel <u>BETTER</u> without using alcohol or other drugs.

Practice

3. People with chemical dependence can't be cured, but they can get _____ .

4. People can do things to feel _____ without using alcohol or other drugs.

Basic Facts Worksheet 3

5. Children usually <u>LOVE</u> their parents, but since alcohol and other drugs affect how people act, think, feel, and treat you, children may not like how their parent <u>BEHAVES</u> when the parent uses alcohol or other drugs.

Practice

5. Children usually _____ their parents, but since alcohol and other drugs affect how people act, think, feel, and treat you, children may not like how their parent _____ when the parent uses alcohol or other drugs.

Basic Facts Worksheet 4

6. When someone is chemically dependent, it's nobody's <u>FAULT</u>.

7. The three **Cs** are:

    1. Children don't <u>CAUSE</u> a parent to develop chemical dependence.

    2. Children can't <u>CONTROL</u> their parent's chemical dependence.

    3. Children can't <u>CURE</u> their parent's chemical dependence.

8. Children from chemically dependent families can:

    1. <u>LEARN</u> the facts about alcohol and other drugs.

    2. Ask for <u>HELP</u> for themselves.

    3. <u>RECOGNIZE</u>, <u>ACCEPT</u>, and <u>SHARE</u> their feelings.

Basic Facts Worksheet 4
Practice

6. When someone is chemically dependent, it's nobody's _____ .

7. The three **C**s are:

    1. Children don't _____ a parent to develop chemical dependence.

    2. Children can't _____ their parent's chemical dependence.

    3. Children can't _____ their parent's chemical dependence.

8. Children from chemically dependent families can:

    1. _____ the facts about alcohol and other drugs.

    2. Ask for _____ for themselves.

    3. _____, _____, and _____ their feelings.

Basic Facts Worksheet 5

9. Feelings aren't good or bad, or right or wrong; they just <u>ARE</u>.

10. Instead of swallowing feelings, it's better to <u>RECOGNIZE</u> them, <u>ACCEPT</u> them, and <u>SHARE</u> them with someone you trust.

Practice

9. Feelings aren't good or bad, or right or wrong; they just _____ .

10. Instead of swallowing feelings, it's better to

_____ them,

_____ them, and

_____ them with someone you trust.

Basic Facts Worksheet 6

11. When children are angry about a problem they can change, they should <u>USE</u> their anger to give them the power to make changes in themselves.

12. When children are angry about a problem they can't change, they should:

    1. <u>ACCEPT</u> what they can't change.
    2. <u>EXPRESS</u> their anger so they can let it <u>GO</u>.
    3. Do something <u>GOOD</u> for themselves.

Practice

11. When children are angry about a problem they can change, they should _____ their anger to give them the power to make changes in themselves.

12. When children are angry about a problem they can't change, they should:

    1. _____ what they can't change.
    2. _____ their anger so they can let it _____ .
    3. Do something _____ for themselves.

187

Basic Facts Worksheet 7

13. Anger management is a way to <u>COPE</u> with anger.

14. The anger management steps are:

    1. <u>RECOGNIZE</u> that you're angry.
    2. <u>ACCEPT</u> your anger.
    3. <u>PRACTICE</u> some <u>RELAXATION</u>.
    4. <u>THINK</u> about ways to express the anger.
    5. <u>EVALUATE</u> the consequences.
    6. <u>CHOOSE</u> the best way.
    7. <u>EXPRESS</u> the anger in a helpful way.

Practice

13. Anger management is a way to _____ with anger.

14. The anger management steps are:

    1. _____ that you're angry.
    2. _____ your anger.
    3. _____ some _____.
    4. _____ about ways to express the anger.
    5. _____ the consequences.
    6. _____ the best way.
    7. _____ the anger in a helpful way.

Basic Facts Worksheet 8

15. Children can't <u>FIX</u> their parent's problems.

16. Children can take <u>GOOD CARE</u> of themselves.

17. Children should <u>WAIT</u> until a chemically dependent parent is sober before talking about how they feel.

Practice

15. Children can't _____ their parent's problems.

16. Children can take _____ of themselves.

17. Children should _____ until a chemically dependent parent is sober before talking about how they feel.

189

Basic Facts Worksheet 9

18. Children from chemically dependent families are more likely to develop chemical dependence than are other children, unless they make <u>GOOD DECISIONS</u>.

19. Children need to take care of their <u>BODIES</u>, their <u>FEELINGS</u>, their <u>MINDS</u>, and their <u>CHOICES</u>.

Practice

18. Children from chemically dependent families are more likely to develop chemical dependence than are other children, unless they make _____.

19. Children need to take care of their _____, their _____, their _____, and their _____.

Basic Facts Worksheet 1

1. Chemical dependence is a <u>DISEASE</u>.

2. Alcohol and other drugs affect how people <u>ACT</u>, <u>THINK</u>, and <u>FEEL</u>, and how people <u>TREAT</u> you.

Practice

1. Chemical dependence is a <u>DISEASE</u>.

2. Alcohol and other drugs affect how people <u>ACT</u>, <u>THINK</u>, and <u>FEEL</u>, and how people <u>TREAT</u> you.

Basic Facts Worksheet 2

3. People with chemical dependence can't be cured, but they can get <u>BETTER</u>.

4. People can do things to feel <u>BETTER</u> without using alcohol or other drugs.

Practice

3. People with chemical dependence can't be cured, but they can get <u>BETTER</u>.

4. People can do things to feel <u>BETTER</u> without using alcohol or other drugs.

Basic Facts Worksheet 3

5. Children usually <u>LOVE</u> their parents, but since alcohol and other drugs affect how people act, think, feel, and treat you, children may not like how their parent <u>BEHAVES</u> when the parent uses alcohol or other drugs.

Practice

5. Children usually <u>LOVE</u> their parents, but since alcohol and other drugs affect how people act, think, feel, and treat you, children may not like how their parent <u>BEHAVES</u> when the parent uses alcohol or other drugs.

Basic Facts Worksheet 4

6. When someone is chemically dependent, it's nobody's <u>FAULT</u>.

7. The three **C**s are:

    1. Children don't <u>CAUSE</u> a parent to develop chemical dependence.

    2. Children can't <u>CONTROL</u> their parent's chemical dependence.

    3. Children can't <u>CURE</u> their parent's chemical dependence.

8. Children from chemically dependent families can:

    1. <u>LEARN</u> the facts about alcohol and other drugs.

    2. Ask for <u>HELP</u> for themselves.

    3. <u>RECOGNIZE</u>, <u>ACCEPT</u>, and <u>SHARE</u> their feelings.

Basic Facts Worksheet 4

Practice

6. When someone is chemically dependent, it's nobody's FAULT.

7. The three **Cs** are:

    1. Children don't CAUSE a parent to develop chemical dependence.

    2. Children can't CONTROL their parent's chemical dependence.

    3. Children can't CURE their parent's chemical dependence.

8. Children from chemically dependent families can:

    1. LEARN the facts about alcohol and other drugs.

    2. Ask for HELP for themselves.

    3. RECOGNIZE, ACCEPT, and SHARE their feelings.

Basic Facts Worksheet 5

9. Feelings aren't good or bad, or right or wrong; they just <u>ARE</u>.

10. Instead of swallowing feelings, it's better to <u>RECOGNIZE</u> them, <u>ACCEPT</u> them, and <u>SHARE</u> them with someone you trust.

Practice

9. Feelings aren't good or bad, or right or wrong; they just <u>ARE</u>.

10. Instead of swallowing feelings, it's better to <u>RECOGNIZE</u> them, <u>ACCEPT</u> them, and <u>SHARE</u> them with someone you trust.

Basic Facts Worksheet 6

11. When children are angry about a problem they can change, they should USE their anger to give them the power to make changes in themselves.

12. When children are angry about a problem they can't change, they should:
    1. ACCEPT what they can't change.
    2. EXPRESS their anger so they can let it GO.
    3. Do something GOOD for themselves.

Practice

11. When children are angry about a problem they can change, they should USE their anger to give them the power to make changes in themselves.

12. When children are angry about a problem they can't change, they should:
    1. ACCEPT what they can't change.
    2. EXPRESS their anger so they can let it GO.
    3. Do something GOOD for themselves.

Basic Facts Worksheet 7

13. Anger management is a way to <u>COPE</u> with anger.
14. The anger management steps are:
    1. <u>RECOGNIZE</u> that you're angry.
    2. <u>ACCEPT</u> your anger.
    3. <u>PRACTICE</u> some <u>RELAXATION</u>.
    4. <u>THINK</u> about ways to express the anger.
    5. <u>EVALUATE</u> the consequences.
    6. <u>CHOOSE</u> the best way.
    7. <u>EXPRESS</u> the anger in a helpful way.

Practice

13. Anger management is a way to <u>COPE</u> with anger.
14. The anger management steps are:
    1. <u>RECOGNIZE</u> that you're angry.
    2. <u>ACCEPT</u> your anger.
    3. <u>PRACTICE</u> some <u>RELAXATION</u>.
    4. <u>THINK</u> about ways to express the anger.
    5. <u>EVALUATE</u> the consequences.
    6. <u>CHOOSE</u> the best way.
    7. <u>EXPRESS</u> the anger in a helpful way.

Basic Facts Worksheet 8

15. Children can't <u>FIX</u> their parent's problems.

16. Children can take <u>GOOD CARE</u> of themselves.

17. Children should <u>WAIT</u> until a chemically dependent parent is sober before talking about how they feel.

Practice

15. Children can't FIX their parent's problems.

16. Children can take GOOD CARE of themselves.

17. Children should WAIT until a chemically dependent parent is sober before talking about how they feel.

Basic Facts Worksheet 9

18. Children from chemically dependent families are more likely to develop chemical dependence than are other children, unless they make <u>GOOD DECISIONS</u>.

19. Children need to take care of their <u>BODIES</u>, their <u>FEELINGS</u>, their <u>MINDS</u>, and their <u>CHOICES</u>.

Practice

18. Children from chemically dependent families are more likely to develop chemical dependence than are other children, unless they make <u>GOOD DECISIONS</u>.

19. Children need to take care of their <u>BODIES</u>, their <u>FEELINGS</u>, their <u>MINDS</u>, and their <u>CHOICES</u>.

1

Chemical dependence
is a
DISEASE.

2

Alcohol and other drugs affect how people <u>ACT</u>, <u>THINK</u>, and <u>FEEL</u>, and how people <u>TREAT</u> you.

3

People
with
chemical dependence
can't be cured,
but they can
get <u>BETTER</u>.

4

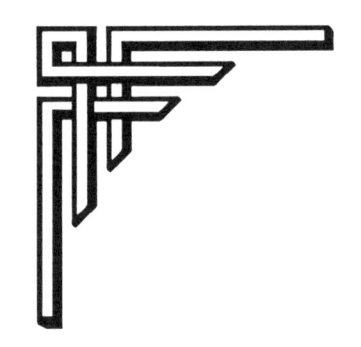

People
can do things
to feel
BETTER
without using
alcohol or other drugs.

5

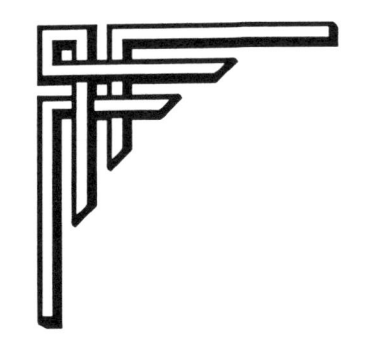

Children usually
<u>LOVE</u> their parents,
but since alcohol
and other drugs
affect how people
act, think, feel, and treat you,
children may not like
how their parent <u>BEHAVES</u>
when the parent uses
alcohol or other drugs.

6

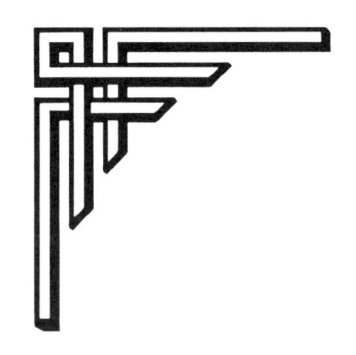

When someone is chemically dependent, it's nobody's FAULT.

7

The three Cs are:

Children don't <u>CAUSE</u> a parent to develop chemical dependence.

Children can't <u>CONTROL</u> their parent's chemical dependence.

Children can't <u>CURE</u> their parent's chemical dependence.

8

Children from chemically dependent families can:

LEARN the facts about alcohol and other drugs.

Ask for **HELP** for themselves.

RECOGNIZE, **ACCEPT**, and **SHARE** their feelings.

9

Feelings aren't
good or bad,
or right or wrong;
they just
<u>ARE</u>.

10

Instead of swallowing feelings, it's better to RECOGNIZE them, ACCEPT them, and SHARE them with someone you trust.

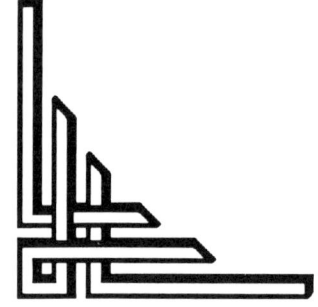

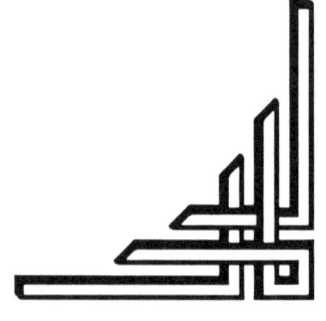

11

When children
are angry
about a problem
they can change,
they should
USE their anger
to give them
the power
to make changes
in themselves.

12

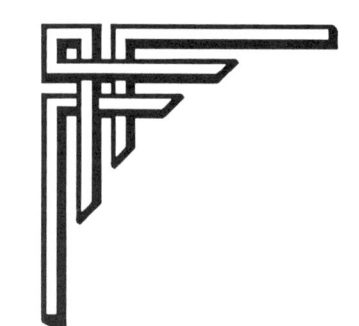

When children are angry about a problem they can't change, they should:

ACCEPT what they can't change.

EXPRESS their anger so they can let it GO.

Do something GOOD for themselves.

13

Anger management
is a way to
<u>COPE</u>
with anger.

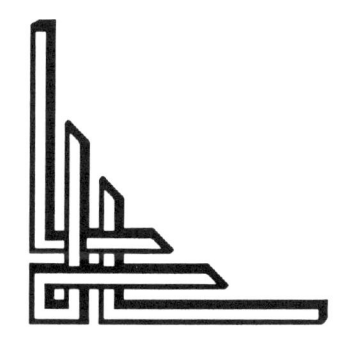

14

The anger management steps are:

<u>RECOGNIZE</u> that you're angry.

<u>ACCEPT</u> your anger.

<u>PRACTICE</u> some <u>RELAXATION</u>.

<u>THINK</u> about ways to express the anger.

<u>EVALUATE</u> the consequences.

<u>CHOOSE</u> the best way.

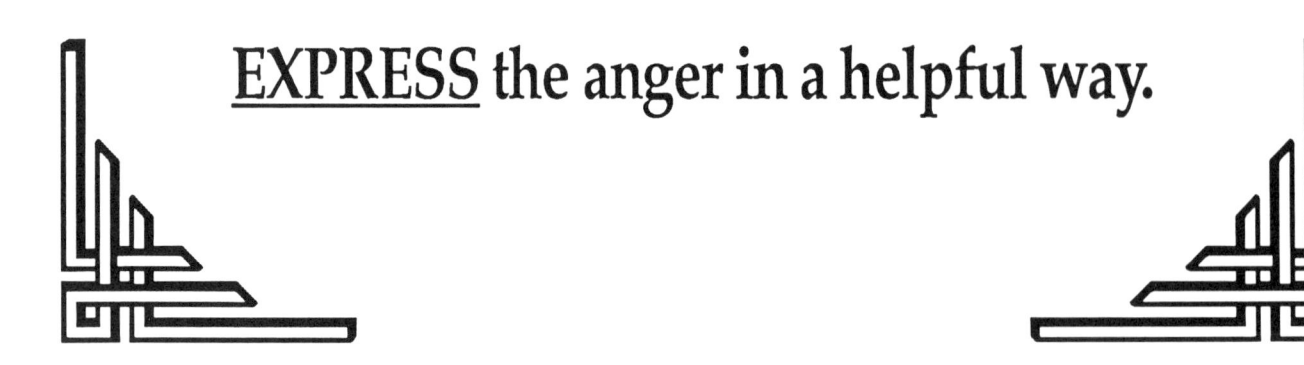

<u>EXPRESS</u> the anger in a helpful way.

15

Children can't
<u>FIX</u>
their
parent's problems.

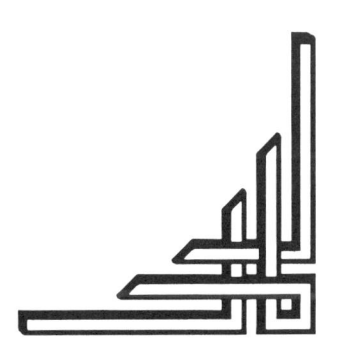

16

Children
can take
GOOD CARE
of themselves.

17

Children should
<u>WAIT</u>
until a
chemically dependent
parent is sober
before
talking about
how they feel.

18

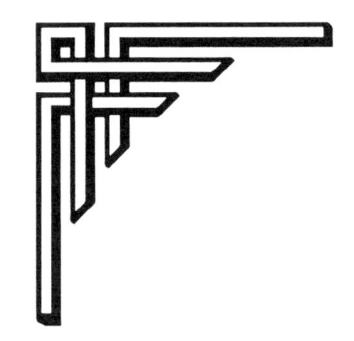

Children from chemically dependent families are more likely to develop chemical dependence than are other children, unless they make <u>GOOD DECISIONS</u>.

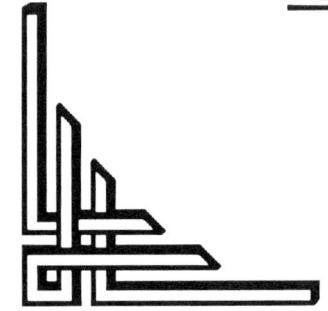

19

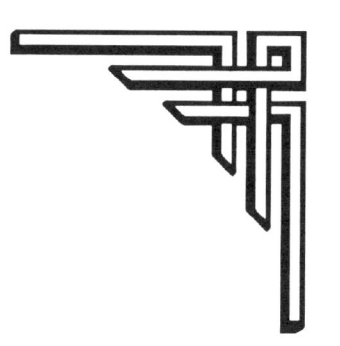

Children need to take care of their <u>BODIES</u>, their <u>FEELINGS</u>, their <u>MINDS</u>, and their <u>CHOICES</u>.

All the Basic Facts

1. Chemical dependence is a DISEASE.
2. Alcohol and other drugs affect how people ACT, THINK, and FEEL, and how people TREAT you.
3. People with chemical dependence can't be cured, but they can get BETTER.
4. People can do things to feel BETTER without using alcohol or other drugs.
5. Children usually LOVE their parents, but since alcohol and other drugs affect how people act, think, feel, and treat you, children may not like how their parent BEHAVES when the parent uses alcohol or other drugs.
6. When someone is chemically dependent, it's nobody's FAULT.
7. The three **Cs** are:
   1. Children don't CAUSE a parent to develop chemical dependence.
   2. Children can't CONTROL their parent's chemical dependence.
   3. Children can't CURE their parent's chemical dependence.
8. Children from chemically dependent families can:
   1. LEARN the facts about alcohol and other drugs.
   2. Ask for HELP for themselves.
   3. RECOGNIZE, ACCEPT, and SHARE their feelings.
9. Feelings aren't good or bad, or right or wrong; they just ARE.
10. Instead of swallowing feelings, it's better to RECOGNIZE them, ACCEPT them, and SHARE them with someone you trust.
11. When children are angry about a problem they can change, they should USE their anger to give them the power to make changes in themselves.
12. When children are angry about a problem they can't change, they should:
    1. ACCEPT what they can't change.
    2. EXPRESS their anger so they can let it GO.
    3. Do something GOOD for themselves.
13. Anger management is a way to COPE with anger.
14. The anger management steps are:
    1. RECOGNIZE that you're angry.
    2. ACCEPT your anger.
    3. PRACTICE some RELAXATION.
    4. THINK about ways to express the anger.
    5. EVALUATE the consequences.
    6. CHOOSE the best way.
    7. EXPRESS the anger in a helpful way.
15. Children can't FIX their parent's problems.
16. Children can take GOOD CARE of themselves.
17. Children should WAIT until a chemically dependent parent is sober before talking about how they feel.
18. Children from chemically dependent families are more likely to develop chemical dependence than are other children, unless they make GOOD DECISIONS.
19. Children need to take care of their BODIES, their FEELINGS, their MINDS, and their CHOICES.

Audience Evaluation Form

1. The most interesting thing I learned from this presentation was_____
_____

2. How much impact do you think this presentation will have on your use of alcohol or other drugs? (circle one)

             None   Some   Much

In what way?
_____
_____

If you're interested in being in a group like Peter the Puppy because you have concerns about someone's use of alcohol or other drugs, please sign here. We will keep your name confidential, but will contact you about your concern soon.

Name: _____

Home room number or Teacher's name: _____

Grade and school you will attend next year: _____

Group Evaluation Form

1. What did you like best about this group?
   _____
   _____

2. What did you like least about this group?
   _____
   _____

3. What do you think should be done differently?
   _____
   _____

4. What would have made the group more helpful to you?
   _____
   _____

5. What do you think is the most important thing you learned from this group?
   _____
   _____

6. What is one good thing that's happened to you because you were in this group?
   _____
   _____

7. As a result of being in this group, how have you changed?
   _____
   _____

Forms

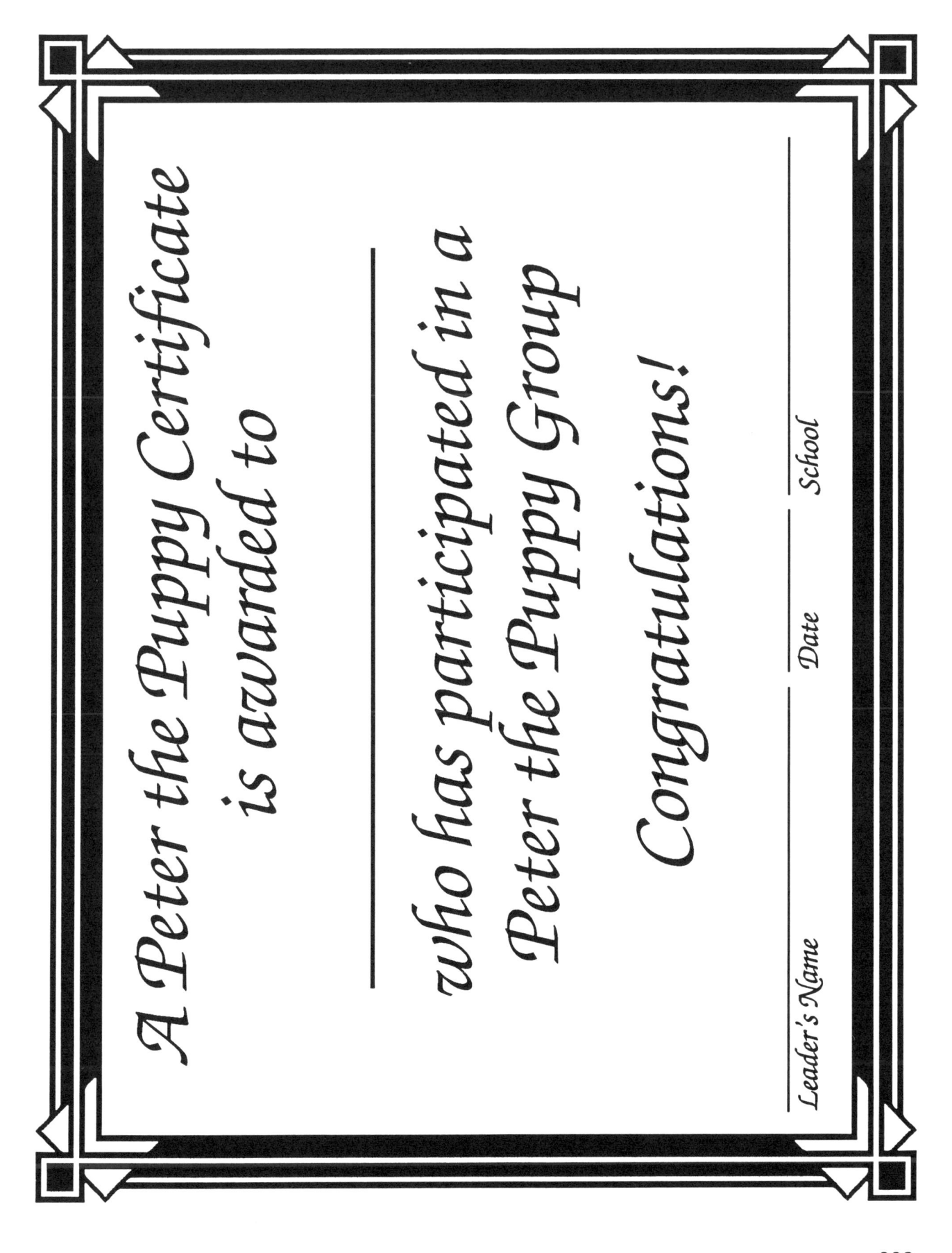

A Peter the Puppy Certificate is awarded to

_____

who has participated in a Peter the Puppy Group

Congratulations!

_____ _____ _____
Leader's Name *Date*   *School*

223

Group Award Badge

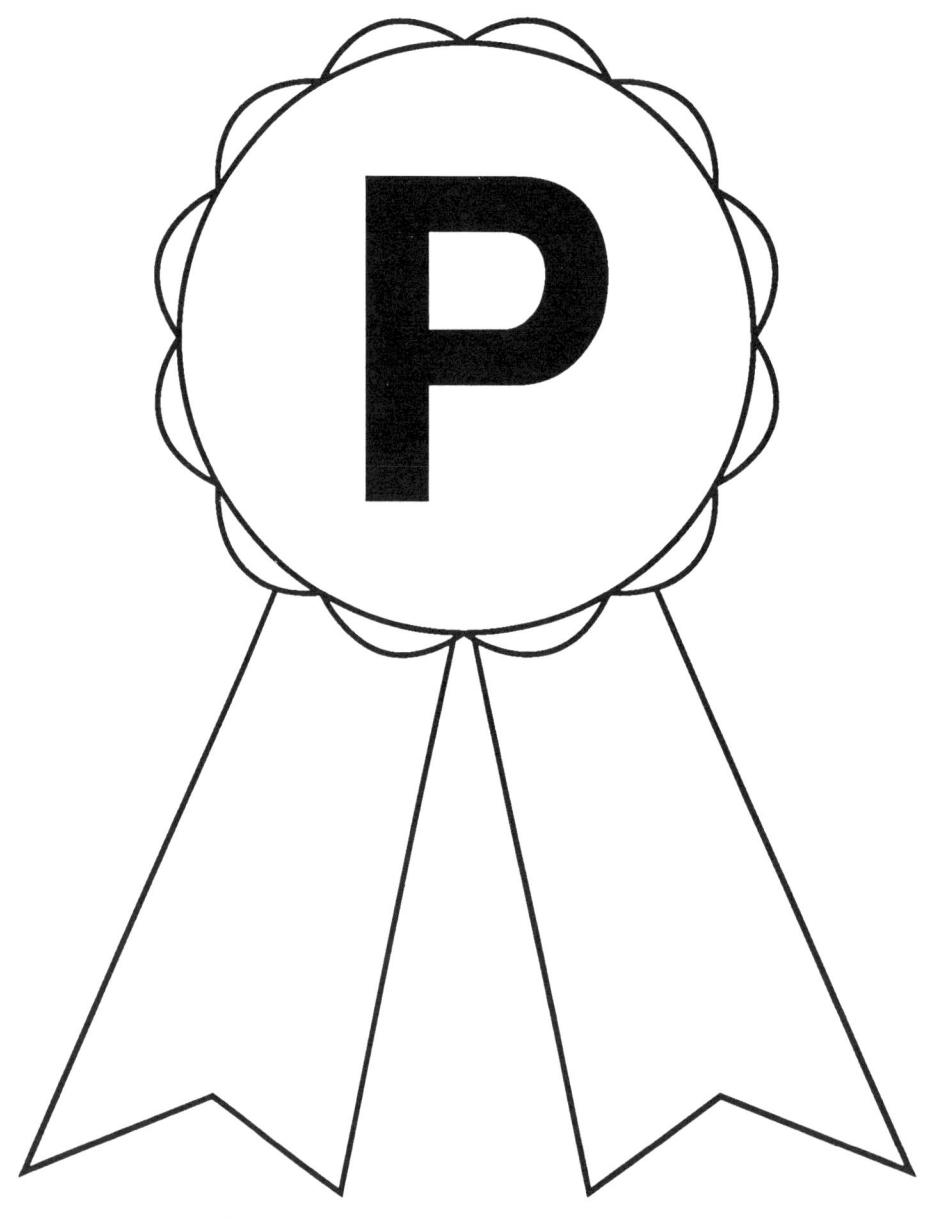

1. Cut out a 2-inch circle of felt.
2. Glue rickrack around the circle's edge.
3. Use rickrack or a marker to put the initial (first letter) of the child's first name in the center of the circle.
4. With tape or glue, attach two 4-inch lengths of blue or red ribbon to the back of the circle.
5. Use tape to attach a safety pin to the back of the circle so the child can wear the badge.

Process and Progress Form

Leader's Name:_____ Session #:_____ Date:_____

Children (group members) present:
_____
_____

Processing the Session

1. What were the objectives of this session?
   _____

2. How were they met?
   _____

3. What concepts must the leader understand to facilitate this session effectively?
   _____

4. What happened during the session?

   Highs:
   _____

   Lows:
   _____

5. What did you see as your strengths as you facilitated this session?
   _____

6. What changes would you make for the next time?
   _____

Noting Progress:

_____
_____

Progress Notes

Group: _____

Members of Group: _____

_____

Session 1:   Date: _____

Notes: _____

_____

_____

Session 2:   Date: _____

Notes: _____

_____

_____

Session 3:   Date: _____

Notes: _____

_____

_____

Session 4:   Date: _____

Notes: _____

_____

_____

Session 5:   Date: _____

Notes: _____

_____

_____

Session 6: Date: _____

Notes: _____

_____

_____

Session 7: Date: _____

Notes: _____

_____

_____

Session 8: Date: _____

Notes: _____

_____

_____

Session 9: Date: _____

Notes: _____

_____

_____

Session 10: Date: _____

Notes: _____

_____

_____

Session 11: Date: _____

Notes: _____

_____

_____

Self-Referral Group Survey Form

Dear Student,

The Pupil Services Staff of *(Name of School)* is very pleased to offer three fun and exciting groups that you can join. These groups will meet once a week during the school day for eleven weeks. Group meetings last about 45 minutes.

Look at the list of groups below. Put an "X" by the group or groups you would like to join. If you think you'd like to be in more than one group, please number them in priority.

_____   Peter the Puppy Group (If you're worried about someone who's using alcohol or other drugs.)

_____   Thomas Barker Group (If you belong to a family that's separated or divorced, has only one parent, or has a stepparent.)

_____   Della the Dinosaur Group (If you or someone close to you uses harmful ways to show anger.)

Name _____

Teacher _____

We'll meet with you soon to talk about the group(s) you chose.

Thank you,

(Signatures of program coordinator, group leader, guidance counselor, and/or school social worker)

Parental Consent Letter

Dear Parent,

As part of our Substance Abuse Prevention Program, the Pupil Services Staff of *(Name of School)* will be offering children a chance to take part in a special group process called *Peter the Puppy Talks About Chemical Dependence in the Family*.

This group will teach group members: (1) the basic facts about alcohol and other drugs; (2) the effects of chemical dependence on the family; (3) how to identify feelings; (4) how to manage anger; (5) coping strategies; (6) how to set personal goals; and (7) how to develop a support system.

The group will be held during the regular school day. It will be led by *(Name of leader and necessary credentials)*. As a teaching technique, we like to have the children make a presentation about what they've learned.

Unless we hear otherwise from you, we'll assume we have your permission for your child to participate in the group. Please know that we treat all information with the strictest confidentiality and the highest respect. If you have any questions or concerns about the group, please call me at *(phone number)*.

We think that the group will be an exciting and positive experience for your child, and we're happy to be able to offer it.

Thank you for your cooperation and participation.

Sincerely,

(Signature of school social worker.)

Screening Interview Outline

Use this outline to screen prospective group members.

Name: _____ Date: _____

Age: _____ Date of Birth: _____

Grade: _____ Teacher's Name: _____

Home Address: _____

Phone: _____

Feelings about school: _____
_____

School adjustment: _____
_____

Who lives in the house with the child? _____
_____

If parents divorced, where does each live? _____
_____

Visitation? _____

What does the child do after school? _____
_____

Typical daily schedule: _____
_____

Hobbies, clubs, sports: _____
_____

Strengths: _____
_____

Weaknesses: _____
_____

Stresses in life: _____
_____

References and Suggested Readings

Ackerman, R. 1983. *Children of alcoholics: A guidebook for educators, therapists, and parents.* Holmes Beach, FL: Learning Publications, Inc.

Beattie, M. 1987. *Co-dependent no more.* San Francisco: Harper/Hazelden.

Black, C. 1981. *It will never happen to me.* Newport Beach, CA: ACT.

Cermak, T. 1985. *A primer on adult children of alcoholics.* Pompano Beach, FL: Health Communications.

Cork, M. 1969. *The forgotten children.* Toronto: Alcoholism and Drug Addiction Research Foundation.

Deutch, C. 1982. *Broken bottles, broken dreams.* New York: Teachers College Press.

Drew, T. 1986. *Getting them sober.* Vol. 3. South Plainfield, NJ: Bridge Publishing.

Henderson, R., and S. B. Blume. 1984. *Children of alcoholics: A review of the literature.* Children of Alcoholics Foundation.

Hunter, M. 1983. *Mastery teaching.* El Segundo, CA: TIP Publications.

Kalter, N. 1990. *Growing up with divorce.* New York: The Free Press.

Kritsberg, W. 1985. *The adult children of alcoholics syndrome.* Pompano Beach, FL: Health Communications.

Leite, E., and P. Espeland. 1987. *Different like me.* Minneapolis: Johnson Institute.

Lerner, H. 1985. *The dance of anger.* New York: Harper & Row.

McGinnis, E., and A. P. Goldstein. 1984. *Skill-streaming the elementary school child.* Champaign, IL: Research Press Company.

Morehouse, E. 1987. Counseling adolescent children of alcoholics in groups, in *Growing in the shadow,* ed. R. Ackerman. Pompano Beach, FL: Health Communications.

National Association for Children of Alcoholics Project. 1987. *Children of alcoholics: Meeting the needs of the young COA in the school setting.* South Laguna, CA: National Association for Children of Alcoholics.

O'Gorman, P., and P. Diaz. 1987. *Breaking the cycle of addiction.* Pompano Beach, FL: Health Communications.

Piaget, J. 1928. *Judgment and reasoning in the child.* New York: Harcourt, Brace, Jovanovich.

Rogers, R., and C. S. McMillan. 1988. *Don't help: A guide to working with the alcoholic.* Seattle: Madison Publishers.

Saunders, A., and B. Remsberg. 1984. *The stress proof child.* New York: Holt Rinehart and Winston.

Schaefer, Dick. 1987. *Choices and consequences: What to do when a teenager uses alcohol/drugs.* Minneapolis: Johnson Institute.

Seixas, J. 1979. *Living with a parent who drinks too much.* New York: Greenwillow Books.

Seixas, J., and G. Youcha. 1985. *Children of alcoholism: A survivor's manual.* New York: Harper and Row.

Typpo, M., and J. Hastings. 1984. *An elephant in the living room.* Minneapolis: CompCare.

Wegscheider, S. 1978. *The family trap.* Crystal, MN: Nurturing Networks.

_____. 1980. *Another chance: Hope and health for the alcoholic family.* Palo Alto, CA: Science and Behavior Books.

Weisinger, H. 1985. *Dr. Weisinger's anger work-out book.* Syracuse, NY: Evaluation Research Associates, Inc.

Woititz, J. G. 1983. *Adult children of alcoholics.* Pompano Beach, FL: Health Communications.

Woodside, M. 1986. *Children of alcoholics: Breaking the cycle.* Journal of School-Health. 56 (Dec.) 448 - 49.

Resources for Help

COAF
Children of Alcoholics Foundation, Inc.
P.O. Box 4185
Grand Central Station
New York, NY 10163
(212) 754-0656

Johnson Institute
7205 Ohms Lane
Minneapolis, MN 55439-2159
1-800-231-5165
(612) 831-1630

NACoA
National Association for Children of Alcoholics
31582 Coast Highway, Suite B
South Laguna, CA 92677
(714) 499-3889

NCADD
National Council on Alcoholism and Drug Dependence
12 West 21st Street
New York, NY 10010
(212) 206-6770